International Perspectives on Employee Engagement

Employee engagement, or more specifically how to obtain more engagement and what to do with the disengaged, preoccupies C-level executives, human resources professionals, and consultants. Factiva, a global database of more than 33,000 national and international publications indexed by Dow Jones, registered a near-continuous double-digit growth in interest in the topic since 1994. COVID-19 appears to be straining work systems, and employee engagement may be suffering.

Interestingly, the American preoccupation with employee engagement, as evidenced by the tens of thousands press mentions indexed by Factiva and the over 38,000 website hits for the search term "employee engagement tools", does not appear shared by the rest of the world.

International Perspectives on Employee Engagement offers a predominately non-American view of employee engagement. The authors address employee engagement from a variety of perspectives. They represent both empirical research and theoretical discussions. The chapters have a distinctly international viewpoint with authors hailing from Europe, Middle East, Africa, and North America. Given the cultural diversity of the authors, this book offers a unique, non-American perspective on employee engagement.

With a new introduction that specifically examines the possible key performance indicators (KPIs) for the annual executive performance appraisal process resulting from the COVID-19 pandemic, the chapters in this book were originally published as a special issue of *International Studies of Management & Organization*.

Michael Segalla is Professor of Management at HEC Paris, France. He is Franco-American and has taught at McGill University and City University of New York, and was appointed Visiting Chair Professor at Hangzhou Dianzi University, China. His research focuses on cross-cultural risk analysis.

International Perspectives on Employee Engagement

Edited by
Michael Segalla

Routledge
Taylor & Francis Group

LONDON AND NEW YORK

First published 2021
by Routledge
2 Park Square, Milton Park, Abingdon, Oxon, OX14 4RN

and by Routledge
605 Third Avenue, New York, NY 10158

Routledge is an imprint of the Taylor & Francis Group, an informa business

British Library Cataloguing-in-Publication Data
A catalogue record for this book is available from the British Library

ISBN13: 978-0-367-69604-7 (hbk)
ISBN13: 978-0-367-69605-4 (pbk)
ISBN13: 978-1-003-14249-2 (ebk)

Typeset in Times LT Std
by codeMantra

Publisher's Note
The publisher accepts responsibility for any inconsistencies that may have arisen during the conversion of this book from journal articles to book chapters, namely the inclusion of journal terminology.

Disclaimer
Every effort has been made to contact copyright holders for their permission to reprint material in this book. The publishers would be grateful to hear from any copyright holder who is not here acknowledged and will undertake to rectify any errors or omissions in future editions of this book.

Contents

Citation Information

The following chapters were originally published in the *International Studies of Management and Organization*, volume 49, issue 1 (2019). When citing this material, please use the original page numbering for each article, as follows:

For any permission-related enquiries please visit:
http://www.tandfonline.com/page/help/permissions

Contributors

Jennifer R. Burnett Senior Principal, Thought Leadership and Advisory Services, Cornerstone OnDemand.

Angelo DeNisi A.B. Freeman School of Business, Tulane University, New Orleans, USA.

Graham Dietz Durham Business School, Durham University, UK.

Timothy C. Lisk Senior Assessment Manager, Cornerstone OnDemand.

Merja Miettinen Kuopio University Hospital, Finland.

Vincent Onyemah Babson College, Babson Park, USA. IPADE Business School, Universidad Panamericana, Mexico.

Lea Rutishauser University of Lucerne, Switzerland.

Hanna Salminen Faculty of Management and Business, Tampere University, Finland.

Asta Savanevičienė School of Economics and Business, Kaunas University of Technology, Lithuania.

Michael Segalla Department of Management and Human Resources, HEC Paris, France. School of Automation, Hangzhou Dianzi University, China.

Anna Sender University of Lucerne, Switzerland.

Živilė Stankevičiūtė School of Economics and Business, Kaunas University of Technology, Lithuania.

Shiva Taghavi Neoma Business School, Mont-Saint-Aignan, France.

Mika Vanhala LUT School of Business and Management, LUT University, Lappeenranta, Finland.

The COVID-19 Crisis – International Perspectives on Employee Engagement

Michael Segalla

INTRODUCTION

Employee engagement has never been more important to firms than during the COVID-19 pandemic. Lock downs around the world place incredible strain on firms and their employees through social distancing practices, employee health and well-being, layoffs, partial work schedules, and work from home policies. Consequently, one should expect that employee engagement will suffer. Because experts predict that the crisis will not end soon, companies need to seriously consider developing and implementing employee relations strategies that support employees and help retain their engagement.

To explore this issue and identify how firms are approaching this problem many of the authors of the papers in this book, along with academics attending the 35 Annual EIASM Strategic Human Resource Management Workshop, contributed to the development of a questionnaire which was distributed to a convenience sample of HR specialists, academics, organizational consultants, and the social networks of our schools. This survey was based on the results of interviews conducted in July and August with C-level executives from industries that are best positioned to use work from home employment models such as banking, software development, consulting, and venture capital. The interviews yielded six COVID-19-specific key performance indicators (KPIs) that firms could, should, and perhaps would use to evaluate the performance of executives, managers, and supervisors of work from home employees. These are Employee Health, Employee Happiness, Maintaining Employee Performance, Controlling Employee Cost, Enhancing Customer Experience, and Deployment of Digital Tools. These KPIs can be used to supplement, or even replace entirely, the traditional performance indicators that firms used in the pre-pandemic period.

Having identified these potentially useful KPIs we developed an online questionnaire to examine whether the academic and business communities were considering implementation of new employee evaluation procedures due to the pandemic. We were especially interested in the pandemic's consequences on employee engagement. We asked our respondents to offer their professional opinions regarding the importance of each of the six KPIs as well as their opinion concerning how employers and employees in their country viewed them. The results, while limited in scope due to the nature of our small convenience sampling, are striking.

COVID-19 KPIs

The pandemic has deeply hurt employers and employees across many economic sectors and geographic zones. Empirical evidence suggests that the most important concern of employees is their physical safety,[1] and this is followed by worry for their economic insecurity.[2] Employee Health due to COVID-19 could be measured by the number of employees who contract the virus, the number of sick days lost, results from depression assessments, the number of employee "burn outs" as reported by a firm's company doctor or psychologist, the number of suicides among employees, and other such indicators. Executives, managers, and supervisors who can help their subordinates avoid these negative outcomes could be rewarded accordingly.

The results of our survey echo the concern about physical safety. The experts in our sample indicated that protecting employee health is extremely important and should be a firm's top priority. (Chart 1) This is unsurprising. What is a bit surprising is that in the opinion of our respondents, the average citizen and the typical firm in their country are less convinced that it is extremely important.

Employee Happiness due to COVID-19 could be measured by better retention rates of valuable employees, better employee engagement as measured by surveys, good team spirit or other happiness indicators measured by regular "pulse polls", or attendance and feedback to online events such as cooking or fitness classes with popular personalities. Executives, managers, and supervisors who can keep their subordinates happy could be rewarded accordingly.

The experts in our survey respondents indicated that Employee Happiness is important, but less so than Employee Health. (Chart 2) They believe that some citizens and companies rate Employee Happiness as either slightly important or not at all important. This might be

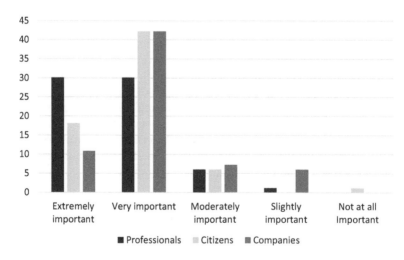

Chart 1   How important is Employee Health?

(N = 56, Percentages)

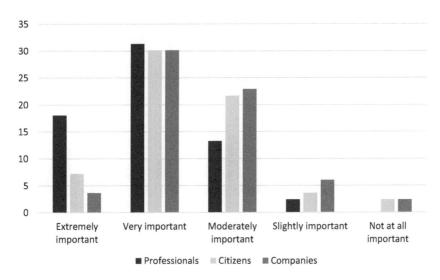

Chart 2 How important is Employee Happiness?

(N = 54, Percentages)

explained by the preponderance of European and Middle Eastern respondents to the survey. As noted later in this book, the concern for Employee Engagement appears to be much lower outside of Anglo-Saxon regions.

Employee Performance could be measured using traditional tools appropriate for their normal work tasks. Companies could also install software solutions that could track employee workflow where applicable. Accurately determining the performance of work from home employees might also require rethinking what constitutes good performance and how it could be better measured. Executives, managers, and supervisors who can better motivate and improve their subordinate's productivity could be rewarded accordingly.

Overall, the survey found that maintaining employee performance during the pandemic was more important to companies and professionals than to average citizens. (Chart 3) However, a national survey of American adults by Morning Consult found that the pandemic is altering the expectations of remote workers.[3] The study reports that respondents were attracted by the comfort and enjoyment of working from home and even believed they were more productive. It appears that there might be a trade off between employee comfort and enjoyment and employee productivity.

Controlling Employee Costs due to COVID-19 could be measured by meeting pre-COVID-19 budget projections, reducing overtime, making employees redundant, freezing new hiring, encouraging early retirement, outsourcing certain tasks, increasing the use of low-paid interns, or other such actions. Executives, managers, and supervisors who can minimize their unit labour costs could be rewarded accordingly.

The respondents indicated that controlling employee costs is not be the priority for professionals, citizens, or firms. Although it should be noted that firms did rank this KPI as extremely important more than the other two groups. This lower level of concern may be due to what is perceived as a relatively short period of difficulty because the lockdowns were relatively short (or almost non-existent in certain European countries). Another factor is most certainly

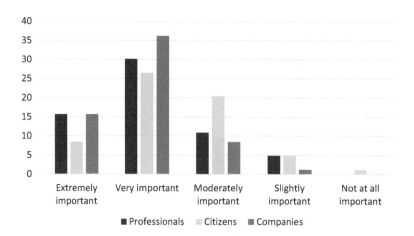

Chart 3   How important is maintaining Employee Performance?

(N = 51, Percentages)

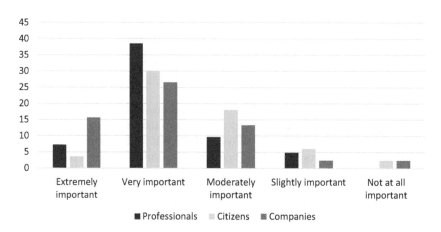

Chart 4   How important is controlling Employee (HRM) Cost?

(N = 50, Percentages)

the financial support many governments provided to firms. The fact that many of the professionals responding to the survey held protected university-affiliated jobs (and therefore faced little or no financial insecurity) may also have contributed to this result. The question faced by most firms however is how important will controlling employee costs become as the pandemic continues to force closures of businesses. Labour expenses are typically one of the largest parts of total operating expenses, especially for labour-intensive and labour-dependent industries. A recent study found that HR professionals spend less than 15% of their time-managing labour costs.[4] Attracting, engaging, and developing top talent is their top priority. The lower level of concern we found is therefore unsurprising increases our confidence that our small sample represents a larger population (Chart 4).

Enhancing Customer Experience during the COVID-19 lockdowns, especially for sales and service employees, may need to be measured and improved. Making a sales call from a work from home environment could be challenging for employees with poor workspaces in their homes. Making sure that customers are happy with the professionalism of your employees is important. Employee training, customer surveys, feedback polls, reviewing recorded ZOOM sessions might all offer insights into customer satisfaction. Executives, managers, and supervisors who can maintain or enhance customer experience could be rewarded accordingly.

Our respondents report that enhancing customer experience remains an important factor for evaluating the performance of executives, managers, and supervisors. It does not appear to be more important than controlling employee costs which may be attributed to the probability than most of the respondents were more likely to be customers than accountants. The interviews conducted with the C-level panel of executives uncovered a concern that firms with work from home salespeople could be presenting a bad image if the employee was working from home. An inappropriate background, the coming and going of family members, poor internet connections, distracting noises, poor lighting, or audio equipment all could send an unprofessional message to customers. Ensuring that sales and service professionalism is maintained is likely to become even more important as the pandemic continues (Chart 5).

Deploying Digital Tools during a COVID-19 lockdown might help employees manage the challenges of working from home. These tools might be teleconferencing equipment (upgraded internet access, webcams, headsets, lighting, green screens, etc.). Software tools could also be deployed to measure employee performance or customer satisfaction. Team working tools such as Slack, Yammer, or Teams might also be useful. Providing online training or coaching to employees may also be useful. Executives, managers, and supervisors who can help their subordinates by deploying and using digital tools effectively could be rewarded accordingly.

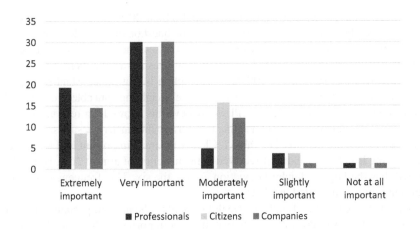

Chart 5   How important is it to Enhance Customer Experience?

(N = 49, Percentages)

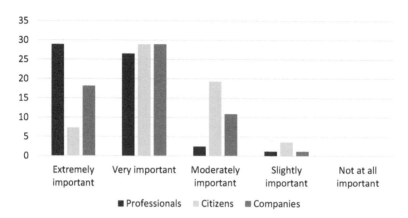

Chart 6   How important is it to Deploy Digital Tools?

(N = 49, Percentages)

Providing the most appropriate tools, now mostly of digital nature, is likely to help employees be healthy, happy, productive, and customer centric. Both our professionals and their reporting about company priorities suggest that deploying digital tools is a recognized response to the short comings of working from home. Evidence that this is widely perceived by firms is easy to find. For example, the share price of Zoom Video Communications was 67 USD at the end of 2019 but was 472 USD at the beginning of October 2020. Other tech companies may have had a less spectacular year but also appear to have generated significant shareholder value (Chart 6).

ANALYSIS AND DISCUSSION

The survey was relatively lengthy and typically took about 20 minutes to complete. During this time our respondents certainly dived deeper into the question of which KPIs were important and to whom. We wanted to give them the opportunity to assess their relative importance so after they completed the questions we inserted a constant sum question asking them to assign a weight (0–100) to each KPI that summed to 100. Our assumption is that the constant sum question is better than a rank ordering because it provides scale level weighting data able to distinguish more precisely the relative importance of each KPI. We believe this allowed our respondents to reconsider their previous evaluations without needing to return to the earlier questions.

The detailed results are displayed in Table 1. Clearly the most important KPI for the respondents is Protecting Employee Health. It received a mean weight of almost 26%. Notice however that this KPI has the largest standard deviation among the six. This frequency distribution of the weighting scores is provided in Chart 7.

It is evident that even though Employee Health is rated as the most important of the six KPIs, not everyone agrees. It is interesting to note that the least important KPI, Controlling Employee Costs, has essentially the same standard deviation with a much larger range.

TABLE 1

Comparative Importance of the Six COVID-19 KPIs

	Minimum	Maximum	Mean	Std. Dev.
Protecting Employee Health Weight	1	50	26.04	11.77
Maintaining Employee Performance Weight	5	40	17.18	6.80
Improving Employee Happiness Weight	1	30	15.92	6.08
Deploying Digital HRM Tools Weight	5	71	15.24	9.98
Enhancing Customer Experience Weight	0	30	13.68	6.42
Controlling Employee Costs Weight	0	85	12.04	11.71

(N=50, Mean of Relative Importance on a 0–100 Scale)

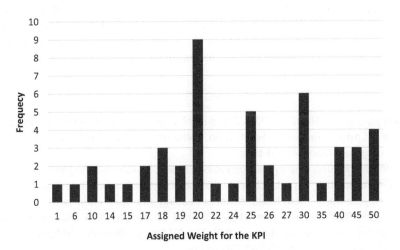

Chart 7   Frequency Distribution of Weights for Employee Health KPI

(N = 50, Frequencies)

Another interesting result is that Maintaining Employee Performance is the second most important KPI with a mean weight of 17. The standard deviation is low compared to employee health and employee costs. Our respondents favour performance over Employee Happiness, but just barely. An important component of Employee Engagement is assumed to be happiness so firms will need to be cautious about placing emphasis on performance during the difficult times of the pandemic.

Finally, the almost complete lack of importance attributed to the Enhancing Customer Experience KPI should be discussed. Notice that this KPI has a very limited range (similar to that of the Employee Happiness KPI) and is never rated above 30. One suspects that not many sales directors or marketing managers responded to the survey. They would have certainly rated this KPI much higher. In fact, during my interviews with the C-level panel of executives the issue of presenting a professional image vis-à-vis customers was often mentioned.

My take away from this survey, which will be ongoing as work from home policies are likely to continue during much of 2021 and perhaps longer, is that companies will need to revisit their performance evaluation systems to insure that they are aligned with new work methods, constraints, and locations. Companies that cannot evolve generally perish. The work from home policies implemented out of necessity in 2020 have given many employees a taste of what was generally reserved for the upper hierarchy of executives. According to many recent surveys, employees like being able to work from home. Perhaps not all the time, but enough that companies will need to ensure that employees have the proper equipment (quality audio, video, lighting, green screens, internet connections, etc.). Firms may also invest in new ways of managing and measuring the work assignments of work from home employees. The sixth KPI, Deploying Digital HRM Tools, ranked in the middle of the pack but had one of the largest ranges. This suggests that the future of work will be ever more tightly managed by software tools. It is only a matter of time until artificial intelligence begins to take an even great role in managing and measuring employees.

The net impact of COVID-19 on employee engagement and the organisation of work is difficult to accurately predict. What is almost a certainty however is that it will be substantial and far-reaching. Firms that are agile and embrace the disruptive energy created by the pandemic are likely to be the survivors best positioned for future success.

NOTES

1. Judge, L. and H. Slaughter. 2020. Failed safe? Enforcing workplace health and safety in the age of Covid-19. Resolution Foundation. 2 November 2020. https://www.resolutionfoundation.org/publications/failed-safe/
2. Feffer, Mark. 2020. Employees worry about, health, finances heading into open enrollment. HCM Technology Report. 22 September 2020. https://www.hcmtechnologyreport.com/employees-worry-about-health-finances-heading-into-open-enrollment/
3. How the Pandemic Has Altered Expectations of Remote Work. 2020. Morning consult. https://go.morningconsult.com/rs/850-TAA-511/images/Remote%20Work%20Report%20-%20Morning%20Consult%20-%20Final.pdf
4. The Biggest Cost of Doing Business: A Closer Look at Labor Costs. 2019. Paycor, Inc. https://www.paycor.com/resource-center/a-closer-look-at-labor-costs

ACKNOWLEDGEMENTS

Many people contributed to this research. First, let me thank the authors of this book. Without their original contributions this chapter would have nothing to introduce. Many of them provided complimentary information about COVID-19 responses in their countries. I would also like to thank the respondents to the survey. Almost every day we are being asked to respond to surveys so when someone does a great service by answering our questions, they deserve my immeasurable thanks. Finally, I would like to thank the executives who advised me and contributed to this survey. Their insights, earned by decades of experience, helped keep the survey focused on the real issues facing our firms and economies. Below is a list of contributors to whom I will be grateful for a long time.

CONTRIBUTORS

Caroline Guillaumin, VP HRM & VP Communications, Société Générale.

David Kellogg, Principal at Dave Kellogg Consulting.

Brigitte Morel-Curran, formerly, Senior Partner Board and CEO practice, Korn Ferry.

Jeff Miller, Chief Learning Officer & VP of Organizational Effectiveness, Cornerstone OnDemand.

Joy Suttles Wolken, VP People & Culture, Alation.

Josefina Gimenez, Research and Inn vation Director, Artimon.

Aleksandra Rudawska, Adjunct Professor, University of Szczecin.

Angelo DeNisi, Professor, A.B. Freeman School of Business, Tulane University.

Nailya Saifulina, Assistant Professor, Universidade de Santiago de Compostela.

Joseph Maidugu, Associate Lecturer, University of Bradford.

José Luis Perea, Doctoral Candidate, University of Cadiz.

Valentin Pfeffer, Doctoral Candidate, EBS Universität für Wirtschaft und Recht.

Beliz Ülgen, Professor, Head of Business Administration Department, Istanbul Commerce University.

Jorge Gomes, Professor, ISEG Universidade de Lisboa.

Lea Rutishauser, Assistant Professor, University of Lucerne.

Monica Santana, Assistant Professor, University of Pablo de Olavide.

Hanna Salminen, Research Specialist, Tampere University & Assistant Professor, University of Vaasa I Kokkola University Center Chydenius, School of Management.

Mika Vanhala, Associate Professor, LUT University, LUT School of Business and Management & Assistant Professor, University of Vaasa I Kokkola University Center Chydenius, School of Management.

Oyku Iyigun, Associate Professor, Ph.D., Istanbul Commerce University.

Ahmet Erkasa, Assistant Professor, Gedik University.

Fadi Alsarhan, Lecturer, iaelyon School of Management/Magellan Research Center – Université Jean Moulin Lyon 3.

Mónica Santana Hernández, Profesora Ayudante Doctora, Departamento de Organización de Empresas y Marketing, Universidad Pablo de Olavide.

Živilė Stankevičiūtė, Associate Professor, School of Economics and Business, Kaunas University of Technology.

Asta Savanevičienė, Principle Researcher, School of Economics and Business, Kaunas University of Technology.

International Perspectives on Employee Engagement: Are American Firms Leading the Way or Walking Alone?

Michael Segalla and Angelo DeNisi

Abstract: This article introduces four types of employee engagement, Active Employee Engagement, Unsatisfied Employee Engagement, No Employee Engagement, and Abusive Employee Engagement. These categories are derived from the diverse literature on employee engagement and through discussions with foreign human resource management scholars. One key assessment of the non-American focused academics is that employee engagement is principally a concern of American businesses. Foreign researchers focus more deeply on creating engagement in the workforce, work groups, and professions.

Employee engagement, or more specifically how to obtain more engagement and what to do with the disengaged, preoccupies C-level executives, human resources professionals, and consultants. Factiva, a global database of more than 33,000 national and international publications indexed by Dow Jones, registered a near continuous double-digit growth in interest in the topic since 1994. Articles mentioning employee engagement skyrocketed in 1998, perhaps due to the launch of Gallup's Q12[1] employee engagement survey. To date, Factiva indexed over 67,000 mentions of employee engagement. Compare this figure with mentions workplace topics such as; workplace diversity (8,833), gender pay gap (42,701), pay for performance (49,950), or work/life balance (155,398), and it appears that this issue is important to America's businesses. The reason may be linked to the attractive correlations between employee engagement levels and customer loyalty, profitability, productivity, turnover, safety incidents, absenteeism, shrinkage, patient safety incidents, and product defects. (Harter et al. 2016) It is unsurprising why this interests American executives.

The volume of these references does not appear to help define what employee engagement means, but whatever it is, it seems good (cf., Macey and Schneider 2008). In one form or another, HR researchers have studied aspects of what is now termed engagement for at least six decades. The heightened interest in this concept over the past two decades may have its origins in the profound changes in worker expectations, but it may also stem from results indicating that engagement can contribute to the corporate bottom line (Harter, Schmidt, and Hayes, 2002), consistent with the corporate shareholder-centric focus of American businesses. Interestingly, American preoccupation with employee engagement, as evidenced by the tens of thousands press mentions indexed by Factiva and the over 38,000 website hits for the search term "employee engagement tools," does not appear shared by the rest of the world (Table 1). Searching the appropriately translated term for employee engagement in Factiva returns hundreds, not thousands, of mentions. Repeating the search in academic journals also produces similar, although not quite so extreme, results (Figure 1). The implication is that employee engagement is mostly an American (perhaps Anglo-Saxon) construct barely

TABLE 1
Articles discussing employee engagement indexed by Factiva.

Language	Term(s)	Factiva hits
English	Terms used for search in English language publications*	
	Employee engagement	61,005
	Total	**61,005**
German	Terms used for search in German language publications*	
	Engagement der Mitarbeiterinnen und Mitarbeiter	329
	Mitarbeiter engagement	659
	Arbeits engagement	88
	Employee engagement	271
	Total	**1,347**
French	Terms used for search in French language publications*	
	L'engagement au travail	80
	L'engagement des collaborateurs	261
	L'engagement des salariés	588
	Employee engagement	43
	Total	**972**
Spanish	Terms used for search in Spanish language publications*	
	El compromiso del empleado	131
	Implicación del empleado	56
	Implicación laboral	99
	Implicación del trabajador	87
	Employee engagement	75
	Total	**448**
Italian	Terms used for search in Italian language publications*	
	Engagement dei dipendenti	40
	Employee engagement	38
	Total	**78**

*The translated terms for employee engagement in German, French, Spanish, and Italian were sourced from articles in magazines, newspapers, and from personal communications with knowledgeable academic researchers from those countries.

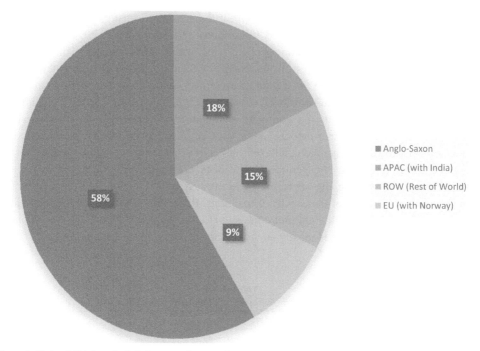

Figure 1 National Origins of scholarly research on employee engagement.

recognized by non-American journalists and researchers. We must note, however, that some scholars have argued that engagement is not really a new concept, but simply a new way of looking at more traditional ideas about the role of positive affect at work (e.g., Newman and Harrison 2008), so that this discrepancy may be more a function of differential labeling rather than differential interest.

This special issue offers a predominately non-American view of employee engagement. The authors address employee engagement from a variety of perspectives. They represent both empirical research and theoretical discussions. The articles have a distinctly international viewpoint with authors hailing from Europe, Middle East, Africa, and North America. The articles are primarily sourced from the EIASM Workshop on Strategic Human Resources[2], which is held annually in Europe. Given the cultural diversity of the authors, the articles offer unique perspectives on employee engagement ranging from employee engagement and sustainable human resource management practices (Stankevičiūtė and Savanevičienė Forthcoming), organizational commitment (Salminen and Miettinen Forthcoming; Onyemah Forthcoming), employee trust and performance (Vanhala and Dietz Forthcoming), employee engagement and the sense of self (Taghavi Forthcoming), to the role of culture, team member exchange, and organizational outcomes (Rutishauser and Sender Forthcoming). There is also an introduction to new digital tools (Burnett and Lisk Forthcoming) for measuring employee engagement, often in near real-time.[3]

TABLE 2
Typology of employee engagement outcomes.

Engagement Quadrants	
No Engagement: Neither employee or employer is engaged in mutual success. Each works only for themselves.	Shared Engagement: Both employee and employer are engaged and actively working for each other's success.
Abusive Engagement: Employer succeeds in creating short-term employee engagement that leads to exhaustion and eventually, burnout.	Unsatisfied Engagement: Engaged employee who perceives no reciprocal engagement from organization

Note: Typology of Engagement proposed by working group attending the HEC Paris / Labex ECODEC workshop on Employee Engagement (see footnote 4).

During a workshop hosted by HEC Paris and Labex EcoDec[4] and subsequent discussions, the invited authors helped to develop a framework for future research on employee engagement. After considerable discussion, especially on the asymmetrical relationship between employee and employer, the group proposed that four types of employee–employer engagement situations should be the focus of future research. These are Shared Engagement, Unsatisfied Engagement, No Engagement, and Abusive engagement Table 2.

Shared Engagement is created when employees create engagement due to their strongly held values. If this intrinsic engagement matches a job and organization that support it, shared engagement can be sustained. However, if a job and organization do not support intrinsic engagement, Unsatisfied Engagement may be the result. The employee is disillusioned and decided to work elsewhere. Unsatisfied Engagement is likely to lead to higher voluntary turnover. The organization loses a productive employee. The third condition is one where the employee is not engaged. Unengaged employees are unlikely to be the most productive and, if they stay in the organization, can potentially create a financial and/or psychological drain on the organization and other employees. The fourth condition is where an employer creates employee engagement but with little employer engagement. This could lead to exhaustion, burnout, or worse, and is Abusive Engagement. These four conditions— Shared Engagement, Unsatisfied Engagement, No Engagement, and Abusive Engagement— are certain to have important effects on the profitability and sustainability of the organization. Therefore, understanding more about the conditions for creating and maintaining engagement and voluntary turnover should be key areas of future study. This is especially appropriate in our current era as the baby boomer generation leaves the labor force as the millennial generation enters. Both appear to have radically different attitudes toward work and organizational commitment.

Employee engagement is an issue that could represent the best interest of employees and the best interests of employers. In its simplest meaning, employee engagement signifies that people who work have a commitment, even perhaps enjoyment, engaging in labor for their organization. This is good for the person—who does not want to enjoy an activity that consumes much of their life—and for the employer—who can count on the best efforts of their employees. This is a classic example of a WIN-WIN relationship. We are happy to introduce our authors and encourage other scholars to build their research findings and theoretical perspectives into future research or corporate policies.

NOTES

1. The Gallup Q12® is a commercial poll that measures 12 elements of employee engagement.
2. European Institute for Advanced Studies in Management (EIASM) is an international network for management research and teaching that includes more than 50,000 management scientists from all over the world.
3. Many firms are competing in this marketplace. For example, Cornerstone OnDemand, a large SAAS HRM talent management firm, is rolling out an employee engagement module targeted toward nearly forty countries.
4. The Labex ECODEC is a research consortium in Economics and Decision Sciences common to three leading French higher education institutions based in the larger Paris area: Ecole Polytechnique, ENSAE, and HEC Paris.

ACKNOWLEDGMENTS

The authors thank EIASM for organizing the Workshop for Strategic Human Resource Management that provided the opportunity to engage in this discussion. We also thank the French Investissements d'Avenir (ANR-11-IDEX-0003/Labex Ecodec/ANR-11-LABX-0047) for funding our working meetings to produce this article. Additionally, we thank HEC Paris School of Management and NEOMA Business School for their support of our research. The corresponding author also thanks Hangzhou Dianzi University for its support during a sabbatical.

REFERENCES

Burnett, J., and T. C. Lisk. Forthcoming. "The Future of Employee Engagement: Real-time Monitoring and Digital Tools for Engaging a Workforce." *International Studies in Management and Organization, Special Issue on International Perspectives on Employee Engagement.*

Harter, J. K., F. L. Schmidt, S. Agrawal, S. K. Plowman, and A. Blue. 2016. "The Relationship between Engagement at Work and Organizational Outcomes." *Gallup Reports* :40.

Harter, J. K., F. L. Schmidt, and T. L. Hayes. 2002. "Business Unit Level Relationship between Employee Satisfaction, employee Engagement and Business Outcomes: A Meta-Analysis." *Journal of Applied Psychology* 87 (2):268–279. doi:10.1037//0021-9010.87.2.268.

Macey, W., and B. Schneider. 2008. "The Meaning of Employee Engagement." *Industrial and Organizational Psychology* 1 (1):3–30. doi:10.1111/j.1754-9434.2007.0002.x.

Newman, D. A., and D. A. Harrison. 2008. "Been There, bottled That: Are State and Behavioral Work Engagement New and Useful Construct "wines"?" *Industrial and Organizational Psychology* 1 (1):31–35. doi:10.1111/j.1754-9434.2007.00003.x.

Onyemah, V. Forthcoming. "What Doesn't Kill You Makes You More Engaged: Rethinking the Link between Organizational Hardship and Organizational Commitment." *International Studies in Management and Organization, Special Issue on International Perspectives on Employee Engagement.*

Rutishauser., L., and A. Sender. Forthcoming. "Effect of Team-Member Exchange on Turnover Intention: A Cross-Cultural Perspective on a Selected Aspect of Employee Engagement." *International Studies in Management and Organization, Special Issue on International Perspectives on Employee Engagement.*

Salminen, H., and M. Miettinen. Forthcoming. "The Role of Perceived Development Opportunities on Affective Organizational Commitment of Older and Younger Nurses." *International Studies in Management and Organization, Special Issue on International Perspectives on Employee Engagement.*

Stankevičiūtė, Z., and A. Savanevičienė. Forthcoming. "Can Sustainable HRM Reduce Work-Related Stress, Work-Family Conflict, and Burnout." *International Studies in Management and Organization, Special Issue on*

International Perspectives on Employee Engagement "Can Sustainable HRM Reduce Work-Related Stress, Work-Family Conflict, and Burnout."

Taghavi, S. Forthcoming. "Mental Construal and Employee Engagement: For more engagement look at the Big Picture." *International Studies in Management and Organization, Special Issue on International Perspectives on Employee Engagement*

Vanhala, M., and G. Dietz. Forthcoming. "How Trust in One's Employer Moderates the Relationship Between HRM and Engagement Related Performance." *International Studies in Management and Organization, Special Issue on International Perspectives on Employee Engagement.*

What Doesn't Kill You Makes You More Engaged: Rethinking the Link between Organizational Hardship and Organizational Commitment

Vincent Onyemah

Abstract: Research has consistently shown that organizational hardship (e.g., role ambiguity and conflict, work overload, organizational injustice) has a negative effect on organizational commitment. However, we posit that receiving help when combatting hardship can reverse that effect. More specifically, employees who face hardship, but receive supervisory support to oppose it, are even more engaged than employees who do not face hardship. These ideas are confirmed by empirical tests on a multinational sample of 2,742 salespeople who participated in a survey, and on a sample of 45 business students who participated in a vignette experiment.

Encountering hardship can make employees want to leave their organization. However, receiving supervisory support to combat this hardship can reverse that effect and sometimes makes employees even more engaged than would otherwise be the case. Under certain circumstances, experiencing hardship might actually increase organizational engagement. Higgins (2006) offers a theoretical framework to explain this effect, positing that the value of a target does not depend solely on the target's subjective hedonic properties, but also on the strength of engagement. A key tenet of this theory is that opposing interfering forces and difficulties increases the strength of engagement, thus increasing the value of the target. In an organizational context, combatting hardship should therefore increase employees' strength of engagement, thus increasing the value they attach to the organization.

Surprisingly, the idea that experiencing hardship can have a positive impact on commitment is absent from research on the antecedents of organizational commitment. In fact, this literature has consistently shown that various manifestations of organizational hardship, such as role ambiguity, role conflict, stress and work overload, organizational injustice, or perceived discrimination, have a negative impact on commitment (e.g., Glisson and Durick 1988; Howell and Dorfman 1981; Hrebiniak and Alutto 1972; Morris and Sherman 1981;

Parasuraman and Alutto 1984; Raja, Johns, and Ntalianis 2004; Sanchez and Brock 1996; Stevens, Beyer, and Trice 1978). In this article, we focus empirically on control system incongruity as a specific case of organizational hardship, but at a theoretical level, we aim to reassess the relationship between organizational hardship and organizational engagement in general, by exploring conditions under which the former can have a positive rather than a negative impact on the latter.

This article contributes to organizational commitment research in several ways. First, this literature has only examined the negative impact of different manifestations of organizational hardship. A necessary next step is to explore the boundary conditions for that impact. In this article, we study one such boundary condition in depth. Specifically, we propose that whether employees oppose organizational hardship is the decisive factor in determining the impact of organizational hardship on organizational commitment. Second, employees might choose not to oppose organizational hardship in the first place, and even when they do, they may give up at some point and/or quit. We argue that receiving supervisory support increases the probability that employees will choose to combat organizational hardship and that they will persevere. Consequently, an examination of whether employees receive supervisory support can refine our understanding of the relationship between organizational hardship and organizational engagement. Finally, we ground our argument in a theoretical framework developed in the social psychology literature (Higgins 2006).

THEORETICAL BACKGROUND AND HYPOTHESES

Organizational Commitment

Employees who are committed to the organization perform better, have lower absenteeism rates, experience greater job satisfaction, and are less likely to leave (e.g., Bateman and Strasser 1984; Mathieu and Kohler 1990; Meyer et al. 1989; Porter et al. 1974; Steers 1977). Thus, organizations have good reason to care about their employees' commitment levels. However, in the age of the boundaryless career (Arthur and Rousseau 1996), characterized by the new psychological contract (Rousseau 1989), organizational commitment is becoming a rare commodity. The new employment relationship requires organizations to foster commitment among their employees without being able to provide guaranteed long-term employment.

Organizational Hardship and Organizational Commitment

We define organizational hardship as employees' perceptions that organization-related factors create an unpleasant work environment, make work conditions difficult, and generally make working in the organization hard to endure. Organizational hardship can appear in many ways, such as role ambiguity, role conflict, stress and work overload, organizational injustice, or perceived discrimination--all factors that have been shown to impact organizational commitment negatively (Mathieu and Zajac 1990; Meyer et al. 2002).

The question arises of what managers can do to alleviate or counteract these negative effects of organizational hardship on organizational commitment. Obviously, one strategy is to work on the cause of hardship itself—to clarify roles, reduce work overload, increase the fairness of organizational procedures, implement antidiscrimination policies, etc. Another strategy focuses on factors that can diminish the negative effects of hardship. For example, perceived control (e.g., Brockner et al. 2004) and fairness (e.g., Brockner et al. 1993) have been shown to reduce the negative impact of layoffs on survivors' organizational commitment.

We take this second strategy one step further by investigating factors that not only diminish, but even reverse the negative effects of hardship. For example, students who want to join fraternities or sororities are often subjected to excruciating initiation rites, which increases their commitment to the group (Cialdini 1993). Research has also shown that organizations can use employees' work-family conflict to increase organizational commitment (Pratt and Rosa 2003). These two cases point to the intriguing possibility that, under some circumstances, experiencing hardship can have a positive effect on commitment. How can this possibility be reconciled with and integrated into the literature on antecedents of organizational commitment? Under what circumstances does organizational hardship positively influence organizational commitment? The purpose of this article is to propose and test answers to these questions.

Higgins (2006, 442) offers a theoretical framework to answer these questions. She conceptualizes value as "not just an experience of pleasure or pain but an experience of the force of attraction toward or repulsion away from something." The intensity of this force is influenced by what Higgins calls the strength of engagement, which refers to the state of being involved in, occupied with, or absorbed by something. A main source of strength of engagement is opposing combating forces or difficulties. In other words, by opposing difficulties, we increase our strength of engagement and ultimately increase the value of a target.

In parallel with Higgins' (2006) conceptualization of value as a force of attraction towards a target, organizational commitment is defined as a force that binds the individual to an organization. It follows that, just as the strength of engagement increases the value of a target, the strength of engagement should increase employees' organizational commitment. Since combatting difficulties increases the strength of engagement, employees who combat organizational hardship are likely to be more engaged and thus more committed to the organization. It is important to emphasize that it is not organizational hardship itself, but combatting it that is the critical factor increasing the strength of engagement and organizational commitment. Employees might choose not to oppose hardship in the first place, and even when they do, they may give up at some point and/or quit (Higgins 2006). In such cases, organizational hardship is likely to have the documented negative impact on organizational commitment.

Hypothesis 1: Organizational Hardship Has a Negative Impact on Organizational Commitment

However, we propose that whether employees oppose hardship is decisive in determining their commitment to the organization. One crucial factor that increases the probability that employees will choose to combat hardship in the first place, and that they will persevere in this opposition, is receiving supervisory support. A supportive supervisor listens to employees' problems, encourages them, appreciates their contributions, and provides valuable feedback (Eisenberger et al. 2002). When facing organizational hardship, employees are likely to seek out their supervisors for help, because they will have a greater need to see that their work is appreciated, they will require more frequent feedback, and they will need to perceive that they can obtain the resources needed to deal with the situation (Sagie and Koslowsky 1994). If they do not receive any support, employees might feel overwhelmed by the hardship they have to endure and become increasingly frustrated with the organization. Yet if employees' requests for help are answered, and they find the necessary support and encouragement, the probability that they will combat the hardship and persevere in this endeavor increases. As noted earlier, opposing hardship increases strength of engagement and thus the value employees attach to the organization. Interestingly, this implies that employees who combat hardship might in fact be even more committed to their organization than employees who face no hardship. This is consistent with the finding that personal investments of time and energy increase the organizational commitment of employees who make such investments (Becker 1960; Meyer and Allen 1984).

Hypothesis 2: Supervisory Support Reverses the Otherwise Negative Impact of Organizational Hardship on Organizational Commitment

Control system incongruity While these hypotheses involve the link between organizational hardship and organizational commitment in general, to test them, we selected a particular case of organizational hardship—control system incongruity. The misconfiguration of control systems constitutes an intriguing form of organizational hardship that has so far been overlooked as a determinant of organizational commitment. Control systems refer to the processes by which "managers direct attention, motivate, and encourage organizational members to act in desired ways to meet the firm's objectives" (Cardinal 2001, 22). The most prevalent classification of control systems distinguishes between behavior-based and outcome-based control systems (e.g., Eisenhardt 1985; Govindarajan and Fisher 1990; Oliver and Anderson 1994; Ouchi 1977; Ouchi and Johnson 1978; Ouchi and Maguire 1975; Turner and Makhija 2006). While behavior-based control refers to monitoring employee activities through direct managerial supervision and company rules, procedures, and standards, outcome-based control focuses exclusively on measuring the results of employees' activities. Control systems consist of several components that can reflect either a behavior- or an outcome-based philosophy. For example, sales force management control systems comprise eight components: focus of performance criteria, number of performance criteria, degree of management intervention, frequency of contact, degree of management monitoring, amount of coaching offered, transparency of evaluation criteria, and compensation scheme (Anderson and Oliver 1987; Anderson and Onyemah 2006; Snell 1992) (see Table 1).

Behavior- and outcome-based control systems are considered the two ends of a continuum, such that a "pure" control system has perfectly aligned elements at the appropriate end of the continuum (Oliver and Anderson 1995). In reality, however, organizations often

TABLE 1
Elements of Outcome- and Behavior-Based Control Systems

	Continuum→	
	Outcome Control (OC)	Behavior Control (BC)
1. Focus of performance criteria. Does management value how sales results are achieved (the effort expended) or simply the results themselves (the outcomes)?	Managers pay particular attention to bottom-line results.	Managers pay particular attention to the methods used to achieve outcomes.
2. Number of performance criteria. Does management judge salespeople using only two or three factors, or does it look at a dozen or more metrics?	Management evaluates a salesperson's performance according to a few observable metrics, primarily market-related such as sales volume.	Management evaluates a salesperson's performance subjectively, using many criteria.
3. Degree of management intervention. Who makes the final decision on important issues related to sales assignments, the salesperson or the manager?	Managers typically offer relatively little supervision. Salespeople make final decisions.	Managers offer relatively heavy supervision and make final decisions.
4. Frequency of contact. Are interactions between salespeople and management easy to enact?	Managers and salespeople have little to no contact.	Managers and salespeople are frequently and extensively in contact.
5. Degree of management monitoring. Does management show serious interest in salespeople's call and activity reports, or are these just a bureaucratic requirement?	Management rarely monitors its sales staff.	Management constantly monitors its sales staff.
6. Amount of coaching offered. Does management suggest ways that salespeople can improve their selling skills and abilities?	Managers offer little to no coaching.	Managers offer frequent, heavy coaching.
7. Transparency of evaluation criteria. How objective, clear, and precise are evaluations at the company?	Evaluation criteria are very transparent.	Evaluation criteria are opaque.
8. Compensation scheme. Is the paycheck based largely on variable compensation triggered by outcomes? Or does it have a large salary component with a performance bonus driven by management's judgments?	A salesperson's compensation is mostly variable, keyed to results.	A salesperson's compensation is mostly fixed, keyed to salary or management's evaluations.

Adapted from Anderson and Onyemah (2006).

employ a combination of control system elements to achieve multifaceted goals (Oliver and Anderson 1995; Turner and Makhija 2006). These combinations can have positive or negative consequences, depending on the structure of the combination (Cardinal 2001; Anderson and Onyemah 2006). Specifically, a congruous control system is a harmonious co-alignment of control system elements; in other words, all elements share the same degree of a behavior

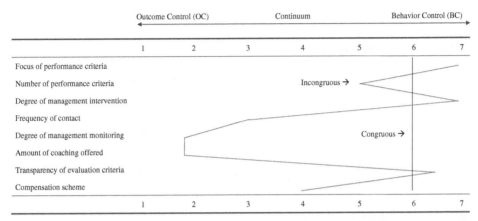

FIGURE 1. Illustration of Incongruous and Congruous Control Systems (adapted from Anderson and Onyemah, 2006)

or outcome based philosophy (Cardinal, Sitkin, and Long 2004; Anderson and Onyemah 2006). Figure 1 graphically illustrates the concept of congruity, and its inverse, incongruity.

Signals emitted by congruous control systems tend to be logical, consistent, and easy for employees to respond to (Anderson and Onyemah 2006). Conversely, an incongruous system inherently sends inconsistent, conflicting signals to employees (Oliver and Anderson 1994). The lack of co-aligned control system elements is detrimental to employee performance because of the confusion, demotivation, and wasted effort they engender. Indeed, employees of organizations with incongruous control systems experience higher role ambiguity and perform less well (Anderson and Onyemah 2006).

STUDY 1

Data Collection and Sample

We tested our hypotheses on an international, cross-industry sample of salespeople. We collected the data via a survey of salespeople working in fifty-one companies based in thirty-eight countries spread across Africa, Asia, Australia, Europe, the Middle East, and North America. The companies operate in various industries, such as chemicals, food, healthcare, information systems and technology, light and heavy engineering, pharmaceuticals, plastics, and services. Each organization provided contact details for all its salespeople. We developed the original questionnaire in English. Via two-way back translations, we obtained six alternative versions of the questionnaire (French, German, Hungarian, Italian, Spanish, Turkish) to cater for those respondents who preferred not to respond (or were unable to respond) in English. First and second-wave mailings yielded 2,742 completed, usable questionnaires (33% female, 67% male). The overall response rate was 75%. On average, respondents were 35 years old with an average work experience in sales of 9 years.

Measures

Control System Incongruity

We measured the eight control system elements (focus of performance criteria, number of performance criteria, degree of management intervention, frequency of contact, degree of management monitoring, amount of coaching offered, transparency of evaluation criteria, and compensation scheme) using multi-item scales (Oliver and Anderson 1994; Onyemah and Anderson 2009). The final scales had an average reliability of 0.78, with alphas ranging from 0.68 to 0.86. To compute control system incongruity, we calculated the standard deviation of the standardized means of the eight elements.

Supervisory Support

This was measured with a scale adapted from Pearce et al. (1992). The scale was highly reliable ($\alpha = 0.93$).

Organizational Commitment

Organizational commitment was measured with seven items (which reflect the affective component) adapted from Porter et al. (1974). The scale was highly reliable ($\alpha = 0.85$).

Control Variables

We controlled for the extent to which the control system reflects a behavior- rather than an outcome-based philosophy. We also controlled for age, education, sales experience, and organizational tenure.

Results

We present the descriptive statistics and correlation matrix of all the variables under consideration in Table 2. The constitutive elements of the control systems as experienced by salespeople were weakly correlated, indicating the existence of control system incongruities.

We display the results of the regression analysis in Table 3. To test the hypotheses, we regressed organizational commitment on control system incongruity, supervisory support, and their interaction. We also included the covariates—age, education, sales experience, organizational tenure, and the degree of behavior based control (excluding them did not change the pattern of results). The model showed a good fit explaining 27.5% of the variance in organizational commitment observed in the data ($F(8,2260) = 107.21, p < 0.01$).

All hypothesized relationships were supported by the data. In support of Hypothesis 1, control system incongruity alone had a negative impact on organizational commitment ($\beta = -0.31, p < 0.001$). However, in support of Hypothesis 2, supervisory support reversed this otherwise negative impact of control system incongruity on organizational commitment.

TABLE 2
Correlations, Means, and Standard Deviations of Variables, Study 1

Variables	M	SD	1	2	3	4	5	6	7	8	9	10	11	12	13	14	15	16
1 Relative importance of input and output factors during evaluation	0	1	1															
2 Number of performance criteria	0	1	0.35	1														
3 Amount of intervention from management	0	1	-0.20	-0.05	1													
4 Amount of contact with management	0	1	0.38	0.11	-0.27	1												
5 Amount of monitoring by management	0	1	0.19	0.09	0.01	0.18	1											
6 Amount of coaching by management	0	1	0.36	0.08	-0.12	0.28	0.62	1										
7 Level of transparency of evaluation criteria	0	1	-0.32	-0.11	0.23	-0.25	-0.36	-0.41	1									
8 Percentage of fixed compensation	0	1	0	0.03	0	0	-0.03	0.02	0.07	1								
9 Degree of behavior-based control	0	0.41	0.59	0.49	0.20	0.48	0.57	0.61	-0.06	0.33	1							
10 Level of control system incongruity	0.94	0.49	-0.04	0.07	0	-0.06	-0.04	-0.06	0.07	0.72	0.21	1						
11 Affective organizational commitment	5.48	1	0.31	0.11	-0.26	0.36	0.34	0.43	-0.36	0	0.31	-0.02	1					
12 Age (years)	35.4	8.02	-0.05	0.05	-0.15	-0.01	-0.14	-0.21	0.03	-0.04	-0.17	0	-0.01	1				
13 Education (years)	11.7	3.83	-0.09	-0.08	0.08	-0.02	-0.01	0	0	-0.01	-0.04	-0.03	-0.04	-0.18	1			
14 General sales experience (years)	8.8	7.86	0.03	0.05	-0.15	0.01	-0.06	-0.12	-0.01	-0.02	-0.08	0.02	0.07	0.72	-0.27	1		
15 Tenure (years)	6.30	6.82	0	0.06	-0.01	-0.03	-0.06	-0.06	0.05	0	-0.02	0	0.05	0.56	-0.28	0.59	1	
16 Supervisory support	4.90	1.18	0.40	0.17	-0.33	0.47	0.33	0.49	-0.42	-0.02	0.37	-0.08	0.46	-0.05	0.02	-0.02	-0.07	1

Variables #1, 2, 3, 4, and 7 were reverse-scored. The underlined correlation coefficients are not significant at $p < 0.05$.

TABLE 3
Results of Regression Analysis, Study 1

	Affective Commitment to the Organization	
	Standardized β Coefficients	t-statistic
Control system incongruity	−0.309***	−4.054
Supervisory support	−0.015	−0.210
Control system incongruity* Supervisory support	0.693***	6.057
Covariates:		
Age	−0.101***	−3.735
Education	−0.006	−0.304
Sales experience	0.121***	4.248
Organizational tenure	0.056*	2.373
Degree of behavior based control	0.097***	4.979
Adjusted R^2	0.275	

$^*p < 0.05.$
$^{***}p < 0.001.$

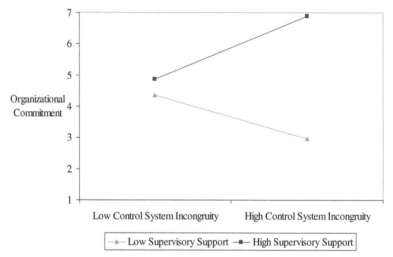

FIGURE 2. Predicted Values of Organizational Commitment as a Function of Control System Incongruity and Supervisory Support, Study 1

Specifically, the interaction coefficient for control system incongruity and supervisory support was positive and greater than the coefficient for control system incongruity ($\beta = 0.69$, $p < 0.001$), demonstrating that control system incongruity had a positive effect on organizational commitment when supervisors were supportive, and a negative effect on organizational commitment when supervisors were not (see Figure 2). In other words, employees were indeed more committed when they faced control system incongruity than when they did not as long as they received supervisory support. It is also interesting that supervisory support alone did not have a significant influence on organizational commitment ($\beta = -0.02$, ns). Instead, our findings suggest that the effect of supervisory support depended on the level of control system incongruity: the greater the incongruity, the greater the effect of supervisory support.

Finally, all covariates, except education, were significant predictors of organizational commitment. While age was negatively related to organizational commitment ($\beta = -0.10$, $p < 0.001$), the remaining covariates were positive: sales experience ($\beta = 0.12$, $p < 0.001$); organizational tenure ($\beta = 0.06$, $p < 0.05$); and degree of behavior-based control ($\beta = 0.10$, $p < 0.001$).

STUDY 2

Purpose of Study 2

The results of Study 1 showed that when employees face organizational hardship in the form of control system incongruity, supportive supervisors can significantly increase employees' commitment levels. The underlying mechanism for this effect of supervisory support is, however, unclear. Consistent with the theoretical framework we used to develop the first set of hypotheses, we propose that supervisory support reverses the otherwise negative impact of control system incongruity on organizational commitment because this support helps employees oppose the hardship imposed by an incongruous control system.

Hypothesis 3: Supervisory Support has a Positive Impact on Organizational Commitment in the Presence of Organizational Hardship because it Helps Employees Combat this Hardship

We tested Hypothesis 3 experimentally in Study 2, while also addressing two other limitations of Study 1: First, Study 1 was correlational, preventing us from making causal inferences; second, the Study 1 dataset contained only salespeople, limiting the generalizability of the results.

Participants, Experimental Design, Procedures, and Materials

Participants were 45 undergraduate business students (25 female, 20 male) at an urban university on the east coast of the United States who participated in the study voluntarily, as part of a business class. The experiment involved a vignette describing a work situation at a fictional company. To ensure participants identified with this situation, we screened them for work experience. All participants had worked prior to their participation in the study, and their cumulative work experience ranged from 3 to 65 months ($M = 25.98$, $SD = 16.19$).

We randomly assigned participants to the experimental conditions. They received e-mails with a link to the online vignette and subsequent questionnaire. They were given one week to complete the questionnaire. The vignette asked participants to imagine that they worked in an organization with an incongruous control system. Depending on the condition, the vignette explained that their supervisor was either non-supportive (non-supportive condition) or supportive (supportive condition).

After reading the vignette, participants filled out an online questionnaire that contained the dependent variable (organizational commitment), the manipulation check, and a scale to test for the hypothesized mediation. Since Study 1 used an organizational commitment scale based on Porter et al. (1974), rather than the more predominant Meyer and Allen (1991) scale, in Study 2 we adapted the Meyer and Allen scale to assess affective organizational commitment. This scale consisted of seven items and was reliable ($\alpha = 0.79$). We checked the manipulation by asking participants to report whether they have a supportive supervisor (same scale as in Study 1; $\alpha = 0.99$). Finally, we included a scale consisting of six items to test the hypothesis that the extent to which the supervisor helps oppose the hardship mediates the effect of supervisory support on organizational commitment. The items included "My supervisor's behavior helps me deal with the problems I encounter in my work," and "I value the assistance my supervisor provides when I face difficulties at work." The "extent to which supervisors help combat hardship" scale was also highly reliable ($\alpha = 0.95$).

Results

Manipulation Check

As expected, participants perceived the supervisor as significantly more supportive in the supportive condition than in the non-supportive condition ($M = 5.89$, $SD = 0.54$ vs. $M = 1.94$, $SD = 0.92$; $F(1, 44) = 317.90$, $p < 0.001$).

Organizational Commitment

As predicted, there was a supportive supervisor main effect, such that participants were more committed to the organization when they had a supportive rather than non-supportive supervisor ($M = 3.40$, $SD = 0.87$ vs. $M = 2.43$, $SD = 0.89$; $F(1, 44) = 13.77$, $p < 0.01$).

The Extent to Which Supervisors Help Combat Hardship as a Mediator

We conducted a mediation analysis based on Baron and Kenny (1986) approach. As shown in Figure 3, and in support of Hypothesis 3, supervisory support predicted organizational commitment ($\beta = 0.49$, $p < 0.01$) as well as the extent to which supervisors help oppose hardship ($\beta = 0.87$, $p < 0.001$); the extent to which supervisors help combat hardship predicted organizational commitment ($\beta = 0.62$, $p < 0.001$); and when supervisory support and the extent to which supervisors help combat hardship simultaneously predicted organizational commitment, only the extent to which supervisors help oppose hardship remained significant ($\beta = 0.79$, $p < 0.01$), whereas supervisory support became insignificant ($\beta = -0.20$, ns). In addition, Sobel's test indicated that the mediation effect of the extent to which supervisors help oppose hardship was indeed significant ($z = 4.73$, $p < 0.001$).

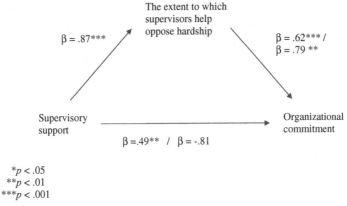

FIGURE 3. The Extent to which Supervisors Help Oppose Hardship as a Mediator, Study 2. $*p < 0.05$; $**p < 0.01$; $***p < 0.001$

DISCUSSION

We hope that our empirical results will prompt organizational commitment scholars to rethink the link between organizational hardship and organizational commitment. Study 1 showed that, although organizational hardship by itself has a negative impact on organizational commitment, supervisory support reverses that effect. Put differently, employees can still have high levels of commitment in the presence of hardship, as long as they receive supervisory support. Study 2 not only replicated this effect, but also confirmed an underlying mechanism—namely, that supervisory support helps employees combat organizational hardship. Consistent with Higgins' (2006) theory of strength of engagement, combatting organizational hardship increases employees' strength of engagement and the value they associate with a certain target, in this case the organization.

The consistency of results across both studies underscores the robustness of our findings. Although both studies have their limitations, the weaknesses of each study are compensated by the strengths of the other. First, Study 1 did not allow us to explore the mechanisms underlying our findings, but Study 2 did. Furthermore, Study 1 was a field study associated with high external validity, whereas Study 2 was a vignette study associated with high internal validity. The experimental design of Study 2 also responds to the call for more studies on organizational commitment with research designs that are better suited to detect causal effects (Meyer et al. 2002). Finally, Study 1 was based on a large and culturally diverse sample, which reinforces its external validity. While we thus incorporated the advice of scholars to conduct studies with employees from a wide variety of organizations (Mathieu and Zajac 1990), the sample was less diverse in terms of work experience as it only contained salespeople. Study 2 contributed to the generalizability of our findings as its sample was not exclusively restricted to salespeople.

This research contributes primarily to the literature on antecedents of organizational commitment. Findings in this literature repeatedly suggest that organizational hardship undermines organizational commitment. In this article, we take a first step towards exploring the conditions under which this negative influence can be reversed. Specifically, we show that when employees receive supervisory support to oppose hardship, they actually become more engaged and thus more committed to the organization. Future research might investigate further conditions under which the otherwise negative effect of organizational hardship on organizational commitment can be reversed. For example, employees might remain committed to the organization despite hardship when they receive other types of support (e.g., peer support), or when they possess certain personality traits (e.g., locus of control, perseverance, optimism, tolerance for ambiguity). Self-efficacy (Bandura 1997) might be a particularly powerful predictor of persistence in combatting hardship.

This research also demonstrates the importance of studying interactions between antecedents of organizational commitment. Previous research has investigated separately the effects of various types of organizational hardship as well as supervisory support, but we know very little about possible interactions between these antecedents. This neglect is regrettable as it limits understanding of what drives organizational commitment. For instance, in Study 1, introducing the interaction term of organizational hardship and supervisory support showed that supervisory support by itself does not have a significant impact on organizational commitment. Instead, supportive supervisors only increase the commitment levels of their subordinates in the presence of hardship, when their effect is sufficiently strong to reverse the otherwise negative impact of hardship itself.

More research is needed, not only to study interactions between antecedents of organizational commitment, but also to examine the mechanisms underlying the effects of these antecedents. Our findings indicate that the help supervisors provide employees to combat hardship constitutes the mechanism underlying the effect of supervisory support on organizational commitment. While we find full mediation for this mechanism, future research might explore additional potential mechanisms. For example, it is conceivable that employees might become more committed to supportive supervisors in the presence of organizational hardship, which in turn would translate into increased commitment to the organization.

Another contribution is the introduction of a variable that has not been empirically studied in the context of organizational commitment–control system incongruity. We, therefore, also contribute to the control system literature by exploring the concept of incongruity and its effects on organizational commitment. Our results highlight the importance of studying control systems, as their configuration represents an interesting property that can significantly affect individual and organizational outcomes.

In this article, we use control system incongruity to operationalize a new, higher level construct: organizational hardship. Future research might explore how other manifestations of organizational hardship, for example bureaucracy, stress and work overload, organizational injustice, or perceived discrimination, interact with supervisory support to determine employee commitment levels.

These findings also contribute to the literatures on leader-member exchange (LMX) theory (Graen and Scandura 1987) and transformational leadership (Bass 1985; Burns 1978). Both LMX and transformational leadership are antecedents of organizational commitment (Bycio, Hackett, and Allen 1995). However, both might also interact with organizational hardship in the same way that supervisory support does. Interestingly, research shows that transformational leaders can make staff perceive stressors as "challenges" rather than "hindrances" (Piccolo and Colquitt 2006; LePine, LePine, and Jackson 2004), which could be a concrete example of how supportive supervisors can help employees combat hardship. As noted in the above discussion on the importance of investigating mechanisms, it would be interesting to shed light on other ways in which supervisors help combat hardship; they might not only do so by reframing hardship, but also by providing the resources to deal with it.

Rethinking the link between organizational hardship and organizational commitment has not only theoretical, but also practical implications. In times of hardship, managers are more likely to distance themselves from their subordinates (Folger and Skarlicki 1998); however, these are the very situations in which their presence is most needed and their impact most powerful (Brockner et al. 1990; Mishra, Spreitzer, and Mishra 1998). We show that when employees receive sufficient supervisory support to combat hardship, they continue to give their best to the organization. This finding should not be taken as an invitation to pay less attention to the creation of a work environment free of organizational hardship. It does, however, emphasize the importance of having good leaders in the organization.

ACKNOWLEDGMENTS

The author thanks EIASM for organizing the Workshop for Strategic Human Resource Management that provided the opportunity to engage in this discussion. We also thank the French Investissements d'Avenir (ANR-11-IDEX-0003/Labex Ecodec/ANR-11-LABX-0047) for funding our working meetings to produce this article. Additionally, we thank HEC Paris School of Management and NEOMA Business School for their support of our research.

REFERENCES

Anderson, E., and R. L. Oliver. 1987. "Perspectives on Behavior-Based versus Outcome-Based Salesforce Control Systems." *Journal of Marketing* 51 (4):76–88. doi: 10.1177/002224298705100407.

Anderson, E., and V. Onyemah. 2006. "How Right Should the Customer Be?" *Harvard Business Review* 84 (7/8): 59–67.

Arthur, M. B., and D. M. Rousseau. 1996. *The Boundaryless Career: a New Employment Principle for a New Organizational Era*. New York: Oxford University Press.

Bandura, A. 1997. *Self-Efficacy: The Exercise of Control*. New York: W. H. Freeman and Company.

Baron, R. M., and D. A. Kenny. 1986. "The Moderator-Mediator Variable Distinction in Social Psychological Research: Conceptual, Strategic, and Statistical Considerations." *Journal of Personality and Social Psychology* 51 (6):1173–82. doi: 10.1037/0022-3514.51.6.1173.

Bass, B. M. 1985. *Leadership and Performance beyond Expectations*. New York: Free Press.

Bateman, T. S., and S. Strasser. 1984. "A Longitudinal Analysis of the Antecedents of Organizational Commitment." *Academy of Management journal. Academy of Management* 27 (1):95–112.

Becker, H. S. 1960. "Notes on the Concept of Commitment." *American Journal of Sociology* 66 (1):32–40. doi: 10.1086/222820.

Brockner, J., R. L. DeWitt, S. Grover, and T. Reed. 1990. "When it is Especially Important to Explain Why: Factors Affecting the Relationship between Managers' Explanations of a Layoff and Survivors' Reactions to the Layoff." *Journal of Experimental Social Psychology* 26 (5):389–407. doi: 10.1016/0022-1031(90)90065-T.

Brockner, J., G. Spreitzer, A. Mishra, W. Hochwarter, L. Pepper, and J. Weinberg. 2004. "Perceived Control as an Antidote to the Negative Effects of Layoffs on Survivors' Organizational Commitment and Job Performance." *Administrative Science Quarterly* 49:76–100.

Brockner, J., B. M. Wiesenfeld, R. Reed, S. Grover, and C. Martin. 1993. "Interactive Effect of Job Content and Context on the Reactions of Layoff Survivors." *Journal of Personality and Social Psychology* 64:187–97.

Burns, J. M. 1978. *Leadership*. New York: Harper and Row.

Bycio, P., R. D. Hackett, and J. S. Allen. 1995. "Further Assessments of Bass's (1985) Conceptualization of Transactional and Transformational Leadership." *Journal of Applied Psychology* 80 (4):468–78. doi: 10.1037/0021-9010.80.4.468.

Cardinal, L. B. 2001. "Technological Innovation in the Pharmaceutical Industry: the Use of Organizational Control in Managing Research and Development." *Organization Science* 12 (1):19–36. doi: 10.1287/orsc.12.1.19.10119.

Cardinal, L. B., S. B. Sitkin, and C. P. Long. 2004. "Balancing and Rebalancing in the Creation and Evolution of Organizational Control." *Organization Science* 15 (4):411–31. doi: 10.1287/orsc.1040.0084.

Cialdini, R. B. 1993. *Influence: The Psychology of Persuasion*. New York: Quill.

Eisenberger, R., F. Stinglhamber, C. Vandenberghe, I. L. Sucharski, and L. Rhoades. 2002. "Perceived Supervisor Support: Contributions to Perceived Organizational Support and Employee Retention." *Journal of Applied Psychology* 87 (3):565–73. doi: 10.1037/0021-9010.87.3.565.

Eisenhardt, K. M. 1985. "Control: Organizational and Economic Approaches." *Management Science* 31 (2):134–49. doi: 10.1287/mnsc.31.2.134.

Folger, R., and D. P. Skarlicki. 1998. "When Tough Times Make Tough Bosses: Managerial Distancing as a Function of Layoff Blame." *Academy of Management Journal* 41:79–87. doi: 10.2307/256899.

Glisson, C., and M. Durick. 1988. "Predictors of Job Satisfaction and Organizational Commitment in Human Service Organizations." *Administrative Science Quarterly* 33 (1):61–81. doi: 10.2307/2392855.

Govindarajan, V., and J. Fisher. 1990. "Strategy, Control Systems, and Resource Sharing: Effects on Business-Unit Performance." *Academy of Management Journal* 33:259–85. doi: 10.2307/256325.

Graen, G. B., and T. A. Scandura. 1987. "Toward a Psychology of Dyadic Organizing." In *Research in organizational behaviour*, edited by L. L. Cummings and B. Staw, vol. 9: 175–208. Greenwich, CT: JAI Press.

Higgins, E. T. 2006. "Value from Hedonic Experience and Engagement." *Psychological Review* 113 (3):439–60. doi: 10.1037/0033-295X.113.3.439.

Howell, J. P., and P. W. Dorfman. 1981. "Substitutes for Leadership: Test of a Construct." *Academy of Management journal. Academy of Management* 24 (4):714–28.

Hrebiniak, L. G., and J. A. Alutto. 1972. "Personal and Role-Related Factors in the Development of Organizational Commitment." *Administrative Science Quarterly* 17 (4):555–73. doi: 10.2307/2393833.

LePine, J. A., M. A. LePine, and C. L. Jackson. 2004. "Challenge and Hindrance Stress: Relationships with Exhaustion, Motivation to Learn, and Learning Performance." *Journal of Applied Psychology* 89 (5):883–91. doi: 10.1037/0021-9010.89.5.883.

Mathieu, J. E., and S. S. Kohler. 1990. "A Test of the Interactive Effects of Organizational Commitment and Job Involvement on Various Types of Absence." *Journal of Vocational Behavior* 36 (1):33–44. doi: 10.1016/0001-8791(90)90013-R.

Mathieu, J. E., and D. M. Zajac. 1990. "A Review and Meta-Analysis of the Antecedents, Correlates, and Consequences of Organizational Commitment." *Psychological Bulletin* 108 (2):171–94. doi: 10.1037/0033-2909.108.2.171.

Meyer, J. P., and N. J. Allen. 1984. "Testing the "Side-Bet Theory" of Organizational Commitment: Some Methodological Considerations." *Journal of Applied Psychology* 69 (3):372–8. doi: 10.1037/0021-9010.69.3.372.

Meyer, J. P., and N. J. Allen. 1991. "A Three-Component Conceptualization of Organizational Commitment." *Human Resource Management Review* 1 (1):61–89. doi: 10.1016/1053-4822(91)90011-Z.

Meyer, J. P., S. V. Paunonen, I. R. Gellatly, R. D. Goffin, and D. N. Jackson. 1989. "Organizational Commitment and Job Performance: It's The Nature of the Commitment That Counts." *Journal of Applied Psychology* 74: 372–8.

Meyer, J. P., D. J. Stanley, L. Herscovitch, and L. Topolnytsky. 2002. "Affective, Continuance, and Normative Commitment to the Organization: A Meta-Analysis of Antecedents, Correlates, and Consequences." *Journal of Vocational Behavior* 61 (1):20–52. doi: 10.1006/jvbe.2001.1842.

Mishra, K. E., G. M. Spreitzer, and A. K. Mishra. 1998. "Preserving Employee Morale during Downsizing." *Sloan Management Review* 39:83–95.

Morris, J. H., and J. D. Sherman. 1981. "Generalizability of an Organizational Commitment Model." *Academy of Management Journal* 24:512–26. doi: 10.2307/255572.

Oliver, R. L., and E. Anderson. 1994. "An Empirical Test of the Consequences of Behavior-And Outcome-Based Sales Control Systems." *Journal of Marketing* 58 (4):53–67. doi: 10.1177/002224299405800405.

Oliver, R. L., and E. Anderson. 1995. "Behavior- and Outcome-Based Sales Control Systems: Evidence and Consequences of Pure-Form and Hybrid Governance." *Journal of Personal Selling and Sales Management* 15: 1–15.

Onyemah, V., and E. Anderson. 2009. "Inconsistencies among the Constitutive Elements of a Sales Force Control System: Test of a Configuration Theory-based Performance Prediction." *Journal of Personal Selling & Sales Management* 29 (1):9–24.

Ouchi, W. G. 1977. "The Relationship between Organizational Structure and Organizational Control." *Administrative Science Quarterly* 22 (1):95–113. doi: 10.2307/2391748.

Ouchi, W. G., and J. B. Johnson. 1978. "Types of Organizational Control and Their Relationship to Emotional Well Being." *Administrative Science Quarterly* 23 (2):293–317. doi: 10.2307/2392566.

Ouchi, W. G., and M. A. Maguire. 1975. "Organizational Control: Two Functions." *Administrative Science Quarterly* 20 (4):559–69. doi: 10.2307/2392023.

Parasuraman, S., and J. A. Alutto. 1984. "Sources and Outcomes of Stress in Organizational Settings: Toward the Development of a Structural Model." *Academy of Management Journal* 27:330–50. doi: 10.2307/255928.

Pearce, J. L., S. M. Sommer, A. Morris, and M. Frideger. 1992. *A Configurational Approach to Interpersonal Relations: Profiles of Workplace Social Relations and Task Interdependence.* Working paper no. OB92015, Irvine: Graduate School of Management, University of California.

Piccolo, R. F., and J. A. Colquitt. 2006. "Transformational Leadership and Job Behaviors: The Mediating Role of Core Job Characteristics." *Academy of Management Journal* 49 (2):327–40. doi: 10.5465/amj.2006.20786079.

Porter, L. W., R. M. Steers, R. T. Mowday, and P. V. Boulian. 1974. "Organizational Commitment, Job Satisfaction, and Turnover among Psychiatric Technicians." *Journal of Applied Psychology* 59 (5):603–9. doi: 10.1037/h0037335.

Pratt, M. G., and J. A. Rosa. 2003. "Transforming Work-Family Conflict into Commitment in Network Marketing Organizations." *Academy of Management Journal* 46:395–418. doi: 10.2307/30040635.

Raja, U., G. Johns, and F. Ntalianis. 2004. "The Impact of Personality on the Psychological Contract." *Academy of Management Journal* 47:350–67. doi: 10.2307/20159586.

Rousseau, D. M. 1989. "Psychological and Implied Contracts in Organizations." *Employee Responsibilities and Rights Journal* 2 (2):121–39. doi: 10.1007/BF01384942.

Sagie, A., and M. Koslowsky. 1994. "Organizational Attitudes and Behaviors as a Function of Participation in Strategic and Tactical Change Decisions: an Application of Path-Goal Theory." *Journal of Organizational Behavior* 15 (1):37–47. doi: 10.1002/job.4030150105.

Sanchez, J. I., and P. Brock. 1996. "Outcomes of Perceived Discrimination among Hispanic Employees: is Diversity Management a Luxury or a Necessity?" *Academy of Management Journal* 39:704–19. doi: 10.2307/256660.

Snell, S. A. 1992. "Control Theory in Strategic Human Resource Management: The Mediating Effect of Administrative Information." *Academy of Management Journal* 35:292–327. doi: 10.2307/256375.

Steers, R. M. 1977. "Antecedents and Outcomes of Organizational Commitment." *Administrative Science Quarterly* 22 (1):46–56. doi: 10.2307/2391745.

Stevens, J. M., J. M. Beyer, and H. M. Trice. 1978. "Assessing Personal, Role, and Organizational Predictors of Managerial Commitment." *Academy of Management Journal* 21:380–96. doi: 10.2307/255721.

Turner, K. L., and M. V. Makhija. 2006. "The Role of Organizational Controls in Managing Knowledge." *Academy of Management Review* 31 (1):197–217. doi: 10.5465/amr.2006.19379631.

How Trust in One's Employer Moderates the Relationship Between HRM and Engagement Related Performance

Mika Vanhala and Graham Dietz*

Abstract: Trust can be seen as important element for the effectiveness of organizational engagement. In particular, in order to be engaged to their work, employees' trust in their employer organization plays a crucial role. This study adopts Dirks and Ferrin's somewhat neglected model of trust as a moderator on the link between human resource management (HRM) and performance. Using a Finnish data-set from a forestry company, we find that trust in the employer moderates the relationship between HRM and unit-level performance. In three out of six HRM practices studied (communication, career opportunities, and job design) the moderation effect was as expected: in a climate where the employer is highly trusted, the effect of the HRM practice on performance was enhanced. However, for three practices (learning and development, performance evaluation and rewards, participation) the effect of HRM was contrary to our hypotheses. We consider the implications of these results for both the trust and HRM literatures, and for HR practitioners.

INTRODUCTION

Trust is very likely to be important for the effectiveness of organizational engagement programs (Chughtai and Buckley 2008), not only in encouraging employees to participate in such initiatives in the first place, but for the program to have a strong effect. In particular, employees need to trust their employer for engagement to work. Chughtai and Buckley have proposed an "upward spiral effect" (2008: 51): high levels of trust in a variety of working relationships boost engagement at work, and engagement subsequently increases trust in working

---

*It is with profound regret to inform our readers that Professor Graham Dietz died during the process of preparing this special issue for ISMO. Graham was an extraordinary scholar and mentor who is deeply missed by the academic community.

relationships. However, as far as we are aware, there are not so many previous studies that have investigated the link between trust and employee work engagement. Trust has been found to explain why some employees are more effectively in completing their jobs than others and also why they go beyond their official tasks, even if there is no notable reward. This kind of effect is very close to the employee engagement which can be characterized by "employees going the extra mile" (see, e.g., Ugwu, Onyishi, and Rodríguez-Sánchez 2014).

Trust itself has been extensively studied, including its antecedents, trust-building processes (Mayer, Davis, and Schoorman 1995; Dirks and Ferrin 2001; Lewicki, Tomlinson, and Gillespie, 2006), and how it might be repaired (Dirks, Lewicki and Zaheer 2009). Other studies have examined the impact of trust on several outcomes, including job satisfaction (Aryee, Budhwar and Chen 2002), the psychological contract between employees and employer (Robinson 1996), and behaviors such as cooperation (De Cremer, Snyder and Dewitte 2001), and team collaboration (Gillespie and Mann 2004—but see Langfred 2004, for a note of caution on trust dynamics in self-managing teams). A handful of studies have reported the decisive impact of trust on employee performance metrics, including improved customer service (Salamon-Deutsch and Robinson 2008) and sales (Davis et al. 2000)—see Colquitt, Scott, and LePine (2007) for a meta-analysis of 132 samples.

There is also a substantial literature on the influence of human resource management (HRM) on a wide range of outcomes. At individual level, in terms of impact on employee attitudes and behaviors, studies have linked HRM to job satisfaction (e.g., Guest 1999), organizational commitment (e.g., Meyer and Smith 2001) and labor turnover (e.g., Batt 2002). Many of these variables have been posited as the mediator in so-called "black box" models of HRM, wherein HRM is understood to shape employees' attitudes and behaviors toward the realization of their employer's strategic aims. These productive attitudes and behaviors are then hypothesized as yielding performance benefits (Purcell et al. 2003). Indeed, there is some evidence of this pathway to organizational effectiveness. At unit and even organizational level, HRM has been linked to performance metrics, including productivity (e.g., Cappelli and Neumark 2001), quality (e.g., MacDuffie 1995), and higher profits and market share (e.g., Huselid 1995; Wright, Gardner and Moynihan 2003)—though the link is disputed (see Schneider et al. 2003). For wide-ranging reviews, see Boselie, Dietz and Boon (2005); Bowen and Ostroff (2004); and Wall and Wood (2005). For a meta-analysis of HRM's impact on performance, based on 92 studies, see Combs et al. (2006).

Despite trust's apparent significance for employees' work-related activities, few studies of the HRM-performance relationship have explored the role of trust (for reviews, see Whitener 1997; Zeffane and Connell 2003; Searle and Dietz 2012). Among those that have looked into the role of trust, a common approach has been to posit a main-effect model: HRM is hypothesized as having a *direct* effect on employees' trust (in whoever the "referent" for the trust is), and employees' trust then serves to mediate the impact of HRM on performance (we review several of these studies shortly). However, the predominance of the main-effect model overlooks a vital but curiously neglected insight revealed by Dirks and Ferrin (2001). After reviewing several major studies of trust, they concluded that trust's influence is more readily apparent as a *moderator* of other relationships, rather than as a direct contributor. Yet surprisingly, this alternative approach to trust remains underdeveloped in the trust literature (we review several moderation studies shortly).

Whether a main-effect or moderation model best accounts for the HRM-performance link is important, because it carries clear implications for the focus of HR efforts: whether that focus should be on HRM's *direct* impact on trust, via the design and implementation of particular policies, or whether HR practitioners should pay more attention to creating a broader "climate" of trust in the organization, aided and abetted by HR policies. Only one study has taken up Dirks and Ferrin's call for such a moderation analysis (Innocenti, Pilati, and Peluso, 2010). We contribute to the literature by supplementing the work of Innocenti and her colleagues with data that extends the impact of HRM into the realm of employee performance and explicitly tests how trust moderates this relationship.

The article proceeds as follows. We first define our central variable of interest, trust, and summarize the two basic models of trust: the main-effect and the moderating effect models. Next, we review the literature on its role in the HRM-performance relationship, highlighting the gap addressed in our study of a Finnish forestry firm. We then present our hypotheses, describe our method and report our findings. In the Discussion, we consider the implications of our results for theory and practice.

THEORETICAL FRAMEWORK

Trust

During the 20 years or so since Mayer et al. (1995) classic conceptualization of trust, a broad consensus has emerged on a three-stage process to trust (McEvily et al. 2003; Colquitt et al. 2007). Trust's antecedents are, firstly, the trusting party's own propensity to trust and, secondly, their assessment of the focal party's trustworthiness. In the influential framework developed by Mayer et al. (1995), three factors are involved when assessing interpersonal trustworthiness: ability (i.e., technical competence), benevolence (i.e., benign motives), and integrity (i.e., adherence to acceptable principles of conduct, such as fair treatment and keeping promises). These three attributes can be translated into manifestations at the organizational level (see Gillespie and Dietz 2009): employees' judgements of "ability" assess the employer's overall effectiveness, as realized via its managers and staff, and evidenced in the reliability and efficiency of its processes, as well as its performance outcomes and access to resources; "benevolence" perceptions reflect an assumption of, and evidence for, benign, or at least non-detrimental, motives on the part of the employer toward its staff, while organizational "integrity" implies consistency between the employer's stated intentions and their actions, as well as an assessment of the organization's moral character, including its commitment to honesty and fair treatment of others. These beliefs, if sufficiently positive, induce "confident positive expectations" (Lewicki, McAllister, and Bies 1998) about the focal party's "intentions or behaviour" (cf. Rousseau et al. 1998: 395) that enable the trustor to render him/herself "vulnerable" to the actions of the focal party. As such, trust is typically viewed as "a psychological state" (Rousseau et al. 1998): a decision, or a judgement call.

Yet there is a final behavioral stage which amounts to demonstration of that trust through a risk-taking act (Dietz and den Hartog 2006; Dietz 2011). For employees in their dealings with their employer, this can include commitment to substantial effort and performance (in the expectation of receiving monetary and non-monetary rewards), as well as loyalty (in the form of a disinclination to quit or to disparage the organization in public), and allowing the employer's representatives to have discretion over something of value, such as one's career.

The Influence of Trust on Work Attitudes and Behaviors

According to Gupta and Kumar (2015; see also Chughtai and Buckley 2008) trust can be conceptualized as an antecedent of employee engagement. The social exchange theory (Blau 1964) can explain the relationship between trust and employee engagement: if employees trust organization they work for, they will be more willing to work harder compared to those who do not trust. In other words, engagement of the employees can be seen as a way they reciprocate or refund to the trustworthiness of the employer organization (see, e.g., Ugwu et al. 2014). Marais and Hofmeyr (2013) confirmed the relationship between trust and employee engagement with the result that if employees have negative trust in their employer, it impacts negatively on how they engage with the organization, and vice versa. In addition, also Ugwu et al. (2014) found support for this linkage by discovering that organizational trust is positively related to employee work engagement. According to them, this can be explained by the fact that, when employees trust their employer, they will accordingly respond with positive job behaviors (see also, e.g., Wat and Shaffer 2005).

In a comprehensive 2001 review, Dirks and Ferrin (2001) explored the theory and examined the available evidence for two models for the impact of trust on outcome variables. Much the most common is the main effect model, wherein one party's high trust in another is hypothesized to have a demonstrable direct effect on the outcome variables of interest. The theory behind this is that the extent to which one party trusts another shapes the interactions between them, with a concomitant, direct effect on levels of, for example, engagement, monitoring, support, and risk-taking: "higher levels of trust are expected to result in more positive attitudes, higher levels of cooperation and other forms of work behaviour, and superior levels of performance" (Dirks and Ferrin 2001: 451). Direct-effect models accounted for 90% of published trust studies in Dirks and Ferrin's review sample. Overall, they found that the evidence is "highly supportive" of a main effect model on *attitudes* (such as "engagement"), but found a "weaker and less consistent" effect on *behaviors* and *performance* (2001: 455). They concluded, counterintuitively for the literature, that trust was not shown to have a particularly strong effect on behaviors and performance. Yet Colquitt and colleagues' alternative meta-analysis (2007) found that trust does predict risk-taking–part of our three-stage model outlined above; that trust correlates positively, but weakly, with commitment (2007: 922), and that trust is strongly related to task performance (0.36, $p = 0.05$).

The alternative proposition, that trust acts more as a moderator on the relationship between another independent variable and its outcomes, is a "less developed" research stream (Jarvenpaa, Shaw and Staples 2004; Innocenti et al. 2010). In the moderation model, the theory is that trust "provides the conditions under which certain outcomes, such as cooperation and higher performance, are likely to occur" (Dirks and Ferrin 2001: 450–451). Trust levels affect how parties interpret other parties' past behaviors, and/or how they assess each other's likely future conduct (Dirks and Ferrin 2001: 456):

> Under high trust the action is interpreted positively, but under low trust, the action is more likely to be interpreted negatively. Hence, the individual is acting in response to the partner's actions [in our case, HRM] . . . as opposed to trust directly. Trust shapes the response elicited. (Dirks and Ferrin 2001: 460)

There have been only a few studies of moderation models of trust: Dirks and Ferrin point to Robinson's (1996) study of recruitment, in which psychological contract breaches were found to be buffered by trust; Rousseau and Tijoriwala's (1999) study of employees' reactions to proposed change management initiatives found that trust in management moderated the relationship between the managers' rationale for change and the perceived legitimacy of their logic, and Dirks' own study of U.S. College Basketball (1999) found no direct effect for trust, but that it did moderate between players' motivation and their team processes and even outcomes. For one, in the recent study by Nair and Salleh (2015), it was found that trust moderates the relationship between performance management practices and their outcomes (one of those being employee engagement). Also Chughtai and Buckley (2008) suggest that if there is high levels of trust within organization, employees are more likely to perceive, e.g., more resources in their work environment. Consequently, this would drive them to be more engaged in their work.

De Cremer and Tyler (2007) confirmed in two experimental studies and two field studies that people's cooperation with an authority is enhanced by the authority's demonstration of procedural fairness, and that this effect is moderated by people's trust in the authority, such that when trust is high, the procedural fairness is seen as more meaningful, credible, and valued, and hence has its greatest impact. We expect a similar relationship for HRM: the impact of an organization's HRM will be enhanced if employees trust their employer, and hence impute benign and honest motives to the design and implementation of its HRM policies.

Finally, Grant and Sumanth (2009) explored the impact on performance of prosocial motivations in members of mission-driven organizations such as charities, NGOs, hospitals and universities. In a series of three studies, they confirmed that trust in management moderated the relationship, such that a trusted manager inspired employees to give greater significance to their work, which had a knock-on beneficial impact on performance: "prosocial motivation is more likely to predict performance when trust cues [from managers] signal to employees that their efforts will have a positive impact on beneficiaries" (2009: 940). Grant and Sumanth conclude that a sense of trust in the workplace enables people to focus on "value-producing activities" rather than worrying about their jobs or career, or monitoring managers' activities (2009: 941). We expect a similar interaction effect for HRM: employees who trust their employer will be less likely to question or even resist its HR practices, and more likely to reciprocate with superior performance levels. We now turn to the role of trust in HRM.

HRM and Trust

Employee trust at work can be interpersonal (e.g., with regard to immediate bosses and colleagues: see McAllister 1995; Davis et al. 2000), but also organizational, which is our interest in this article. The main-effect model, wherein employer trustworthiness is hypothesized as being directly influenced by the organization's HRM policies, is the standard approach to analyzing the relationship. Several individual practices have been found to predict levels of trust in a variety of relationships: with senior management (voice mechanisms—Farndale et al. 2011; appraisal—Mayer and Davis 1999; communication, procedural justice, empowerment, and employee development—Tzafrir et al. 2004), and with coworkers (performance measurement, appraisal, pay policies—Pearce, Branyiczki, and Bigley 2000). HRM Systems have also been shown to contribute to perceptions of employer trustworthiness. Tsui et al. (1997; Tsui and Wu 2005) compared four models of "employee-organization relationship," differentiated by the inducements offered by the employer and the employee obligations these sought to invoke. They found that the "mutual investment" approach (an open-ended, long-term social and economic exchange arrangement) delivered the highest levels of trust and the best performance outcomes, although the strictly transactional "quasi-spot contract" model (minimal social engagement but high rewards attached to demanding performance targets) also produced good performance. Gould-Williams (2003, 2004) found support for the hypothesis that HR practices can be a powerful predictor of U.K. local government workers' trust in their employer's systems and in interpersonal trust in the workplace. In both these studies, positive trust levels were associated with beneficial effects on organizational performance. Tzafrir (2005) found that HR managers' trust in their staff predicted investments in HR systems, which in turn had an impact on performance. Whitener (2001) found that trust in management mediates the relationship between perceived organizational support and organizational commitment. She suggested that employee trust is stronger when they perceive that the employer organization is committed to and supportive of them. She also found that trust in management was stronger if organizations conducted developmental appraisals. McCauley and Kuhnert (1992) found out that employee trust in management was associated with job security, performance appraisal, and professional development. They state that professional development (i.e., promotion and career opportunities) may, in fact, be the most important factor in differentiating the level of employee trust in management.

Although researchers recognize that trust in organizations operates at multiple levels (see, e.g., Rousseau et al. 1998), at present there is no clear consensus on the concept of trust within the organization. Increasingly, studies recognize that there is also an impersonal dimension to employee trust in employer organizations (see, for example, McCauley and Kuhnert 1992; Maguire and Phillips 2008; Vanhala, Puumalainen, and Blomqvist 2011), whereby employees trust their top management team as a unit, and their organization as a functional structure (e.g., strategy, vision, and processes). However, research on organizational trust has not typically analyzed trust in employer organizations as distinct from interpersonal trust, nor has the role of that kind of trust been studied comprehensively enough.

We have suggested that this type of organizational trust can be influenced by the HRM practices adopted in the organization.

However, recent theorizing (Gillespie and Dietz 2009) suggests that HRM policies are not the only source of evidence for employer trustworthiness. Other indicators are relevant to employee appraisals of trustworthiness, including the decisions, statements, and actions of senior and line managers; the cultural values espoused and enacted by the organization; the various systems and practices it creates and deploys in order to operate, including its policies for employee welfare and development (i.e., HRM); and, finally, evidence sourced beyond the organization, in the institutions and regulations that govern its activities, and in the reputation it has with wider public audiences (for more detail on organization-level trust, see Gillespie and Dietz 2009). The implication of this is that trust can be hypothesized as moderating the impact of HRM on work-related attitudes and behaviors such as employees' engagement to their work.

The moderation model posits an alternative to the main-effect model. If employees trust their employer in general, they will be expected to adopt benign or, at least, non-cynical interpretations of the intentions behind the employer's HR practices. This should lead to a reciprocal response, in terms of increased employee effort and performance (Rousseau and Tijoriwala 1999; Dirks and Ferrin 2001). By contrast, a moderation model would predict that employees who doubt their employer's motives and/or competence will be less likely to view their employer's HR policies as a positive exchange, which would have a damaging knock-on effect on attitudes and behaviors at work. As we have already discussed, trust levels partly determine how parties interpret other's past behaviors, and/or their likely future conduct (Dirks and Ferrin 2001: 456). As Innocenti and colleagues have suggested, factors beyond the HR sphere of influence can affect employees' general trust perceptions, and may damage or enhance the impact of HRM:

> Any behaviours that run counter to perceptions of support, equity and integration may compromise the effects of [HRM's] "positive chain of influence" [on performance], and reduce or nullify the impact of a company's HRM system. (2010: 11–12)

Theirs is the only study of which we are aware to have tested the moderating effect of trust on HRM and performance. Specifically, Innocenti et al. (2010) posited a moderating effect for "trust in management" on the relationship between an "AMO" style (cf. Appelbaum et al. 2000) configuration of HRM—in which policies influence employees' ability, motivation, and opportunities to utilize their skills and knowledge and participate meaningfully in work-based decisions—and employees' "attitude toward their employer" (a compilation of items on job satisfaction and organizational commitment). Using a sample of 9,166 respondents from the Great Place To Work survey in Italy, with its own measures for each variable, they found that trust did enhance HRM's "motivation"-oriented policies (namely, "non-monetary recognition" and "economic rewards"), but had no effect on the other two elements of HRM: "When trust is high the path from motivation to EAO [Employee Attitudes towards the Organization] is significantly stronger than when trust is low ($t = 3.0$, $p < 0.05$)" (Innocenti et al. 2010: 10).

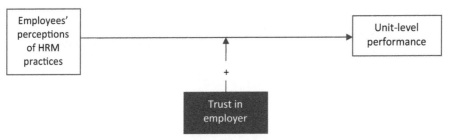

Figure 1. Trust in employer as a moderator of the relationship between perceived HRM and unit-level performance.

Hypotheses

From the above, we argue that employee trust in their employer positively moderates the impact of individual HRM practices on performance. Specifically, the more employees trust their employer, the stronger the effect of HR practices on employee performance. We collapse our six separate hypotheses for each HRM practice into one overall hypothesis as follows:

> Employee trust in their employer positively moderates the relationship between unit-level performance and a) "learning and development," b) "communication," c) "performance evaluation and rewards," d) "career opportunities," e) "participation (i.e., employee voice mechanisms)" and f) "job design."

Figure 1 summarizes the model tested in the study.

METHOD

Data Collection and Sampling

Our analysis is based on a sample of blue-collar workers in a large forestry company in Finland. We collected the data in August-September 2008. Company representatives randomly distributed 700 questionnaires with a covering letter among the firm's 1,400 employees. We received 411 useable responses from eight units in two of the firm's mills (a 58.7% response rate). As shown in Table 1, most of the respondents were men, most had long tenure at the firm, and most had not attended higher education. Our discussions with company representatives and details contained in the firm's annual report confirm that our sample is representative of the whole workforce.

Measures

For all measures and the reliability results, see Appendix 1. All scales were five-point Likert scales (1 = strongly disagree, 5 = strongly agree).

TABLE 1.
Profile of the respondents.

	FORESTRY COMPANY
Gender	
Men	79.3
Women	18
Age	
21–30	7.8
31–40	23.4
41–50	39.9
51–60	25.8
Education	
Vocational education	63
Further education qualification	8.5
Higher education qualification	4.9
Tenure	
<10 years	0.2
11–15 years	14.4
16–20 years	13.6
>20 years	52.3
Job position	
Employees	72.5
'Officials'	14.8
Team Leaders	6.1
Managers	3.6

Independent variable: "Perceived HRM." We adopted and adapted the scale by Delery and Doty (1996). Eighteen items covered six main areas of HRM: learning and development (3 items), communication (3 items), performance evaluation and rewards (3 items), career opportunities (3 items), participation (3 items), and job design (3 items). The respondents indicated the extent to which they strongly agreed or disagreed with the statements describing their perceptions of HRM practices in their organization.

Dependent variables. In this study, we measure performance as the individual employee's subjective perceptions of performance at unit level. This is for two reasons. Firstly, the company was reluctant to share objective performance data and, second, we wanted to ensure comparability between different kinds of organizational units. While perceptual data may introduce limitations through increased measurement error and mono-method bias, research has found that measures of perceived performance do tend to correlate positively with object-ive measures (see Robinson and Pearce 1988; Delaney and Huselid 1996). We measured unit-level performance using four items from Dvir and Shenhar (1992). These cover how one's work-unit copes with new business opportunities and future challenges, as well as the resources of the unit. In other words, our measure for performance is related to how capable the unit is to perform at present and in the future. Based on this, one can make assessment about the unit he/she is working for, and consequently, it will also have an effect to one's engagement to their work.

Moderating variable. We measured "organizational trust" using the seven items developed, tested, and affirmed by Vanhala et al. (2011). The scale is designed particularly to assess employees' trust in their employer as an organization. The items cover the essential attributes of trustworthiness (cf. Mayer et al. 1995), including the organization's resilience, sustainability, and competitiveness (i.e., its ability), positive staff expectations about their own future (i.e., organizational benevolence), and the commitment of the organization and its senior management team to ethical conduct (i.e., integrity). The authors used Confirmatory Factor Analysis on data from 166 respondents with different kinds of organizational backgrounds in Finland to validate the scale (Vanhala et al. 2011).

Control variables. Certain respondent characteristics can influence the relationship between HRM practices and performance (see Tzafrir et al. 2004). We, therefore, controlled for job tenure, classified as under one year, 1–5 years, 6–10 years, 11–15 years, 16–20 years, and over 20 years.

Methods

The data relied on self-report measures, and so common method variance might have biased the findings. We used Harman's one-factor test to control for this (Podsakoff et al. 2003). The largest factor accounted for 31.7% of the variance, which suggests that common method variance bias was not a concern.

The first step was to validate the measurement model, including HRM practices, trust in employer and performance by means of confirmatory factor analysis (CFA). Second, we used structural equation modeling (SEM) to test each hypothesis. We processed 411 cases using LISREL 8.50, and computed the covariance matrix using PRELIS 2.50. We used the maximum likelihood estimation method.

FINDINGS

Measurement Model, Reliability and Correlations

The CFA revealed that the loadings of all the items were high (with the exception of one item in "career opportunities") and statistically significant (see Appendix 1). This means that they were all related to their specified constructs, confirming the posited relationships between the indicators and constructs. In terms of construct reliability and Cronbach's alpha, all concepts exceeded an acceptable level of 0.60, with the exception of "career opportunities" (CR = 0.52; alpha = 0.47).

Table 2 presents the correlation matrix, mean scores, and standard deviations for all the main variables. Note that there are statistically significant positive correlations between them all.

TABLE 2.
Correlation matrix.

Construct	Mean	SD	1	2	3	4	5	6	7	8	9
1. Job tenure	4.96	1.30									
2. Trust in organization	3.16	0.65	−0.023	(0.78)							
3. Unit-level performance	3.69	0.70	0.071	0.530**	(0.75)						
4. Learning and development	3.11	0.90	−0.008	0.593**	0.407**	(0.86)					
5. Communication	3.36	0.80	−0.030	0.571**	0.329**	0.529**	(0.73)				
6. Performance evaluation and rewards	3.08	0.69	0.015	0.573**	0.376**	0.520**	0.509**	(0.69)			
7. Career opportunities	2.97	0.72	0.058	0.562**	0.343**	0.668**	0.472**	0.491**	(0.47)		
8. Participation	2.73	0.84	−0.061	0.538**	0.327**	0.598**	0.490**	0.522**	0.502**	(0.81)	
9. Job design	3.10	0.78	−0.008	0.521**	0.334**	0.629**	0.522**	0.510**	0.506**	0.519**	(0.74)

Cronbach's alphas are presented in parentheses on the diagonal.
**Indicates statistically significant correlation at the 0.01 level.

Analysis

We used structural equation modeling to test our hypotheses. We conducted a multi-group analysis to check whether "trust in employer" moderates the relationship between perceived HRM practice and unit-level performance. We averaged the scores for the items covering trust in employer to obtain a composite indicator of trust. We used a median split (median = 3.14) to divide our respondents into two sub-samples according to their trust score—one with a low level of trust (sample size: 183, mean = 2.58, SD = 0.41) and one with a high level (sample size: 228, mean = 3.62, SD = 0.39).

Next, we tested the models on each sub-group separately in order to check whether the models produced an acceptable fit for each group. Results for the "Low trust model" were as follows: chi-square = 320.68, df = 188, $p = 0.000$, RMSEA = 0.062, GFI = 0.862, NNFI = 0.941, CFI = 0.952, IFI = 0.953. Results for the "High trust model" were as follows: chi-square = 336.11, df = 188, $p = 0.006$, RMSEA = 0.059, GFI = 0.881, NNFI = 0.948, CFI = 0.958, IFI = 0.958. The results of the chi-square tests were not significant. However, this test has been found to be sensitive to sample size, and other tests can be used to assess goodness of fit (see, e.g., Hair et al. 2006). Overall, the indices suggest that the models produced an adequate fit.

We then conducted a multi-group analysis by comparing the two groups associated with different levels of trust. We compared a constrained model against an unconstrained one (see, for example, Hair et al. 2006). In the constrained model, the path from HRM practice to performance was not allowed to vary across the two sub-groups. In the unconstrained model, this path was allowed to freely change across the sub-groups. If the chi-square difference test and other fit indices show that constraining the path weakens the model, the moderation is supported. After this we compared the parameter associated with the relationship between HRM practice and performance. If the parameter is higher in the "high trust" sample the moderation is in the direction hypothesized.

TABLE 3.
Model Comparison

Model	Chi-square (df)	Change in chi-square (df)	RMSEA	GFI	CFI	NNFI	IFI	CAIC
Learning and development								
Unconstrained	175.56 (47)		0.114	0.919	0.871	0.846	0.872	348.024
Constrained	275.83 (49)	100.27 (2)	0.15	0.855	0.749	0.713	0.751	437.26
Gamma$_{LT}$	0.31	Gamma$_{HT}$	0.30					
t	3.32	t	3.27					
Communication								
Unconstrained	174.6 (47)		0.115	0.907	0.798	0.759	0.801	350.066
Constrained	201 (49)	26.4 (2)	0.123	0.892	0.755	0.720	0.758	362.428
Gamma$_{LT}$	0.14	Gamma$_{HT}$	0.41					
t	1.59	3.335	3.35					
Performance evaluation and rewards								
Unconstrained	156.3 (47)		0.107	0.924	0.807	0.77	0.81	331.767
Constrained	186.68 (49)	30.38 (2)	0.117	0.901	0.765	0.731	0.767	348.109
Gamma$_{LT}$	0.37	Gamma$_{HT}$	0.3					
t	3.33	3.335	2.7					
Career opportunities								
Unconstrained	152.73 (47)		0.105	0.911	0.778	0.735	0.782	202.73
Constrained	169.85 (49)	17.12 (2)	0.11	0.903	0.741	0.704	0.745	331.28
Gamma$_{LT}$	0.1	Gamma$_{HT}$	0.42					
t	0.83	t	2.64					
Participation								
Unconstrained	174.73 (47)		0.115	0.926	0.826	0.792	0.828	350.199
Constrained	284.15 (49)	109.42 (2)	0.153	0.841	0.701	0.658	0.704	445.582
Gamma$_{LT}$	0.33	Gamma$_{HT}$	0.13					
t	3.37	t	1.43					
Job design								
Unconstrained	132.89 (47)		0.095	0.938	0.876	0.852	0.877	308.354
Constrained	165.3 (49)	32.41 (2)	0.108	0.925	0.823	0.798	0.825	326.727
Gamma$_{LT}$	0.24	Gamma$_{HT}$	0.36					
t	2.35	t	3.55					

Results

Our results reveal (see Table 3) that "trust in employer" moderates the relationships between all of the HRM practices and unit-level performance. For three practices (Hypothesis 1b: communication; H1d: career opportunities; H1f: job design), the parameter associated with the relationship between HRM practice and performance was as we supposed (i.e., higher in the "high trust" sample). This supported hypotheses 1b, 1d, and 1f. However, for three of the practices (H1a: learning and development; H1c: performance evaluation and rewards; H1e: participation) the parameter associated with the relationship between HRM practice and performance was higher in the "*low trust*" sample. Consequently, we rejected hypotheses 1a, 1c, and 1e. These findings will be discussed in more detail in the Conclusion.

DISCUSSION AND CONCLUSIONS

In this article, we enhance the HRM and trust literatures by studying the moderating role of "trust in employer" in the HRM-performance linkage. This is one of the first studies to do so, and contributes to the growing literature on the role of trust in the context of intra-organizational relationships. In previous studies (Vanhala and Dietz 2015; Vanhala and Ritala 2016) exploring trust's direct and mediating effects, it was found out that, at different levels of performance (individual, unit, and organization levels) as well as at innovativeness of the organization, HRM practices can make a positive impact through the mediation of "trust in employer." This previous study suggested that if HRM practices can be designed specifically to enhance employees' trust in their employer organization, the effect on performance will be positive. In the alternative model presented here, we follow Dirks and Ferrin's (2001) theoretical arguments for trust's role as a moderator. Our results show that for all six HRM practices that we studied, trust in employer moderates the relationship between HRM and unit-level performance. In three HRM practices (communication; career opportunities; job design) the moderation effect of the trust in employer was as we expected: if the employer is perceived as trustworthy, the effect of HRM on performance is positive. These results suggest that the association between these three individual HRM practices and unit-level performance is more effective if employees trust their employer. However, for three other HRM practices (learning and development; performance evaluation and rewards; participation), the moderating effect proved contrary to our hypotheses: the effect of HRM on performance is *greater* when employees trust their employer *less*. These results support Dirks and Ferrin's (2001) arguments in favor of trust as a moderator. Yet the different effects of different policies have implications for theory and practice, which future research will need to address.

One explanation could be that the effect of these latter three practices impact performance less if the organization is greatly trusted. For example, considering "performance evaluation and rewards," it could be that when employees trust the organization, they do not want to compete against each other, and consequently such a policy negatively affects performance, and ultimately their engagement to work). Alternatively, if the organization is highly-structured (as could be assumed in a paper mill), participative decision-making might be less effective in high-trust situations. Another explanation might be that the sequence is the reverse of that depicted by Dirks and Ferrin: HRM brings clarity to the relationship and to the link between employees' work and their unit's performance. In so doing, the determinant [HRM] overcomes a low trust climate to bring benefits to performance.

This does not, however, account for the different effects found for different HR policies. We suggest possible explanations for these individual policy effects. Performance evaluations may be more effective in low-trust environments, because the appraisal may induce fear and pressure, which, from a work intensification perspective (cf. Green 2004), might enhance performance. Contrarily, voice may be viewed by low-trust employees as a valuable counterbalance to the power of their employer, for whose subsequent impact on unit-level performance *employees* can take credit. Our findings for "learning and development" may have a similar explanation: in a low-trust climate, the impact of the HRD may be perceived as within the *employees'* realm of control (i.e., *their* skills and knowledge are being utilized, enhanced, and exploited). In other words, policies controlled primarily by the employer might be most effective in a high-trust climate, whereas policies significantly influenced by employees might be most effective in low-trust conditions. We offer some further thoughts on this below, in addressing the study's limitations.

LIMITATIONS AND FURTHER RESEARCH

One limitation of this study is that we only looked at the relationship between HRM practices and trust with regard to a single referent, the employer. We did so for the theoretical reasons outlined above. However, the role of trust in the relationship between HRM and performance is not limited to trust in the employer. HRM practices can also build interpersonal trust, such as employees' trust in their immediate and senior leaders (Spreitzer and Mishra 1999; Davis et al. 2000); managers' trust in their subordinates (Salamon-Deutsch and Robinson 2008); or trust among colleagues (McAllister 1995). For example, learning and development, and job design, could also affect trust between colleagues. If an employee knows that a system of learning and development is in place, or that jobs are well-designed and there is scope to modify work tasks, they may be more confident in their colleagues' competence. HRM practices also influence trust in supervisors and managers who implement these organization-wide practices. For example, appraisal systems have been found to shape employees' trust in their line and senior managers (Mayer and Davis 1999). The key point here is that employees do not perceive HRM practices in a vacuum. Supervisors and managers implement HRM practices, and employees develop trust in them based on how they behave and act. Even so, HR practices are typically *organization-level* variables, and might be expected to impact on this relationship the most. Nevertheless, future studies could explore multiple interpersonal trust relations, alongside "trust in employer," to see which trust relationships matter, and which are influenced by HRM. Then it would be possible to build and test a model of the relationships between HRM practices, different levels of trust, and performance. A second limitation of this study is that objective measures of performance were not available, and future studies incorporating these would further enhance our understanding of how trust moderates the HRM-performance relationship.

Future research might look into three-way interactions with a mediating "black box" attitude (cf. Grant and Sumanth 2009). Given the meta-analysis finding by Colquitt et al. of a relationship with organizational commitment but, curiously, no relationship with organizational citizenship behavior, these two variables suggest themselves as obvious candidates. Engagement is another candidate, e.g. by testing Chughtai and Buckley's (2008) propositions. In their conceptual article, it is suggested that the direct effect of inter-personal trust (i.e., individual employees' trust in colleagues as well as trust in supervisors/managers) on work engagement should be studied. In addition, they suggest that also the interaction effect of individual's propensity to trust in above mentioned relationship should be taken into account as well.

Finally, Dirks and Ferrin (2001: 461) proposed that future research should investigate the suggestion that "situational strength" (cf. Mischel 1977)—the clarity of cues and institutions governing the relationship between HRM and performance, such as, in our case, a company's HRM practices—might determine whether a main-effect model would be more likely than a moderation model (see also Jarvenpaa et al. 2004). Thus, future research might explore the hypothesis that the moderating effect of "trust in employer" on the relationship between HRM and attitudes such as engagement, and hence on performance indicators, will be greater in organizational settings where the signals sent by the HRM system are of moderate strength.

ACKNOWLEDGMENTS

The authors thank EIASM for organizing the Workshop for Strategic Human Resource Management that provided the opportunity to engage in this discussion. We also thank the French Investissements d'Avenir (ANR-11-IDEX-0003/Labex Ecodec/ANR-11-LABX-0047) for funding our working meetings to produce this article. Additionally, we thank HEC Paris School of Management and NEOMA Business School for their support of our research.

REFERENCES

Appelbaum, E., T. Bailey, P. Berg, and A. Kalleberg. 2000. *Manufacturing Advantage. Why High Performance Work Systems Pay off.* Ithaca, NY: Cornell University Press.

Aryee, S., P. S. Budhwar, and Z. X. Chen. 2002. "Trust as a Mediator of the Relationship Between Organizational Justice and Work Outcomes: Test of a Social Exchanbe Model." *Journal of Organizational Behavior* 23:267–85. doi: 10.1002/job.138.

Batt, R. 2002. "Managing Customer Services: Human Resource Practices, Quit Rates, and Sales Growth." *Academy of Management Journal* 45 (3):587–97. doi: 10.2307/3069383.

Blau, P. 1964. *Exchange and Power is Social Life.* New York, NY: Wiley

Boselie, P., G. Dietz, and C. Boon. 2005. "Communalities and Contradictions in HRM and Performance Research." *Human Resource Management Journal* 15 (3):67–94.

Bowen, D. E., and C. Ostroff. 2004. "Understanding HRM-Performance Linkages: The Role of the "Strength" of the HRM System." *Academy of Management Review* 29 (2):202–21.

Cappelli, P., and D. Neumark. 2001. "Do 'High-Performance Work Practices Improve Establishment-Level Outcomes?" *Industrial and Labor Relations Review* 54 (4):737–75. doi: 10.2307/2696111.

Chughtai, A. A., and F. Buckley. 2008. "Work Engagement and Its Relationship with State and Trait Trust: A Conceptual Analysis." *Journal of Behavioral and Applied Management* 10 (1):47–71.

Colquitt, J. A., B. A. Scott, and L. A. LePine. 2007. "Trust, Trustworthiness, and Trust Propensity: A Meta-Analytic Test of their Unique Relationships with Risk Taking and Job Performance." *Journal of Applied Psychology* 92 (4):909–27. doi: 10.1037/0021-9010.92.4.909.

Combs, J., Y. Liu, A. Hall, and D. Ketchen. 2006. "How Much do High-Performance Work Practices Matter? A Meta-Analysis of their Effects on Organizational Performance." *Personnel Psychology* 59 (3):501–28.

Davis, J. H., F. D. Schoorman, R. C. Mayer, and H. H. Tan. 2000. "The Trusted General Manager and Business Unit Performance: Empirical Evidence of a Competitive Advantage." *Strategic Management Journal* 21 (5): 563–76. doi: 10.1002/(SICI)1097-0266(200005)21:5<563::AID-SMJ99>3.0.CO;2-0.

De Cremer, D., and T. R. Tyler. 2007. "The Effects of Trust in Authority and Procedural Fairness on Cooperation." *The Journal of applied psychology* 92 (3):639–49.

De Cremer, D., M. Snyder, and S. Dewitte. 2001. "The Less I Trust, the Less I Contribute (or Not): Effects of Trust, Accountability and Self-Monitoring in Social Dilemmas." *European Journal of Social Psychology* 31:91–107.

Delaney, J. T., and M. A. Huselid. 1996. "The Impact of Human Resource Management Practices on Perceptions of Organizational Performance." *Academy of Management Journal* 39:949–69. doi: 10.2307/256718.

Delery, J. E., and D. H. Doty. 1996. "Modes of Theorizing in Strategic Human Resource Management: Tests of Universalistic, Contingency, and Configurational Performance Predictions." *Academy of Management Journal* 39: 802–35. doi: 10.5465/256713.

Dietz, G., and D. den Hartog. 2006. "Measuring Trust Inside Organizations." *Personnel Review* 35 (5):557–88. doi: 10.1108/00483480610682299.

Dirks, K. T., and D. L. Ferrin. 2001. "The Role of Trust in Organisational Settings." *Organisational Science* 12 (4): 450–67. doi: 10.1287/orsc.12.4.450.10640.

Dirks, K. T., R. J. Lewicki, and A. Zaheer. 2009. "Repairing Relationships within and between Organizations: Building a Conceptual Foundation." *Academy of Management Review* 34 (1):68–84. doi: 10.5465/amr.2009.35713285.

Dvir, D., and A. Shenhar. 1992. "Measuring the Success of Technology-Based Strategic Business Units." *Engineering Management Journal* 4 (4):33–8. doi: 10.1080/10429247.1992.11414701.

Farndale, E., J. van Ruiten, C. Kelliher, and V. Hope-Hailey. 2011. "The Influence of Perceived Employee Voice on Organizational Commitment: An Exchange Perspective." *Human Resource Management* 50 (1):113–29. doi: 10.1002/hrm.20404.

Gillespie, N., and L. Mann. 2004. "Transformational Leadership and Shared Values: The Building Blocks of Trust." *Journal of Managerial Psychology* 19 (6):588–607. doi: 10.1108/02683940410551507.

Gould-Williams, J. 2003. "The Importance of HR Practices and Workplace Trust in Achieving Superior Performance: A Study of Public-Sector Organizations." *International Journal of Human Resource Management* 14 (1):28–54. doi: 10.1080/09585190210158501.

Gillespie, N., and G. Dietz. 2009. "Trust Repair after an Organization Level Failure." *Academy of Management Review* 34 (1):127–45. doi: 10.5465/amr.2009.35713319.

Gould-Williams, J. 2004. "The Effects of 'High Commitment' HRM Practices on Employee Attitude: The Views of Public Sector Workers." *Public Administration* 82 (1):63–81. doi: 10.1111/j.0033-3298.2004.00383.x.

Grant, A. M., and J. J. Sumanth. 2009. "Mission Possible? The Performance of Pro-Socially Motivated Employees Depends on Managerial Trustworthiness." *Journal of Applied Psychology* 94 (4):927–44. doi: 10.1037/a0014391.

Green, F. 2004. "Why Has Work Effort Become More Intense?" *Industrial Relations* 43 (4):709–41. doi: 10.1111/j.0019-8676.2004.00359.x.

Guest, D. E. 1999. "Human Resource Management: The Workers' Verdict." *Human Resource Management Journal* 9 (3):5–25. doi: 10.1111/j.1748-8583.1999.tb00200.x.

Gupta, M., and Y. Kumar. 2015. "Examining the Mediating Role of Trust in Indian B-Schools." *Asia-Pacific Journal of Business Administration* 7 (1):89–103. doi: 10.1108/APJBA-04-2014-0048.

Hair, J. F., W. C. Black, B. J. Rabin, R. E. Anderson, and R. L. Tatham. 2006. *Multivariate Data Analysis*, 6th ed. New Jersey: Pearson Education.

Huselid, M. A. 1995. "The Impact of Human Resource Management Practices on Turnover, Productivity and Corporate Financial Performance." *Academy of Management Journal* 38 (3):635–70. doi: 10.2307/256741.

Innocenti, L., M. Pilati, and A. M. Peluso. 2010. "Trust as Moderator in the Relationship Between HRM Practices and Employee Attitudes." *Human Resource Management Journal* 21 (3):303–17. doi: 10.1111/j.1748-8583.2010.00151.x.

Jarvenpaa, S. L., T. R. Shaw, and D. S. Staples. 2004. "Toward Contextualized Theories of Trust: The Role of Trust in Global Virtual Teams." *Information Systems Research* 15 (3):250–67. doi: 10.1287/isre.1040.0028.

Langfred, C. 2004. "Too Much of a Good Thing? Negative Effects of High Trust and Individual Autonomy in Self-Managing Teams." *Academy of Management Journal* 47:385–99.

Lewicki, R., D. McAllister, and R. Bies. 1998. "Trust and Distrust: New Relationships and Realities". *Academy of Management Review* 23:438–58. doi: 10.5465/amr.1998.926620.

Lewicki, R., E. C. Tomlinson, and N. Gillespie. 2006. "Models of Interpersonal Trust Development: Theoretical Approaches, Empirical Evidence, and Future Directions." *Journal of Management* 32 (6):991–1022. doi: 10.1177/0149206306294405.

MacDuffie, J. P. 1995. "Human Resource Bundles and Manufacturing Performance: Organizational Logic and Flexible Production Systems in the World Auto Industry." *Industrial and Labor Relations Review* 48 (2): 197–221. Doi 10.1177/001979399504800201

Maguire, S., and N. Phillips. 2008. "'Citibankers' at Citigroup: A Study of the Loss of Institutional Trust After a Merger." *Journal of Management Studies* 45 (2):372–401. doi: 10.1111/j.1467-6486.2007.00760.x.

Marais, A., and K. Hofmeyr. 2013. "Corporate Restructuring: Does Damage to Institutional Trust Affect Employee Engagement." *South African Journal of Labour Relations* 37 (2):9–29.

Mayer, R. C., and J. H. Davis. 1999. "The Effect of the Performance Appraisal System on Trust for Management: A Field Quasiexperiment." *Journal of Applied Psychology* 84 (1): 123–36. doi: 10.1037/0021-9010.84.1.123.

Mayer, R. C., J. H. Davis, and F. D. Schoorman. 1995. "An Integrative Model of Organizational Trust." *Academy of Management Review* 20 (3):709–34. doi: 10.5465/amr.1995.9508080335.

McAllister, D. J. 1995. "Affect- and Cognition-Based Trust as Foundations for Interpersonal Co-operation in Organisations." *Academy of Management Journal* 38 (1):24–59. doi: 10.2307/256727.

McCauley, D. P., and K. W. Kuhnert. 1992. "A Theoretical Review and Empirical Investigation of Employee Trust in Management." *Public Administration Quarterly* 16 (2):265–84.

McEvily, B., V. Perrone, and A. A. Zaheer. 2003. "Trust As an Organizing Principle." *Organization Science* 14 (1): 91–103. doi: 10.1287/orsc.14.1.91.12814.

Meyer, J., and C. Smith. 2001. "HRM Practices and Organisational Commitment: Test of a Mediation Model." *Canadian Journal of Administrative Science* 17 (4):319–31. doi: 10.1111/j.1936-4490.2000.tb00231.x.

Mischel, W. 1977. "On the Future of Personality Measurement." *American Psychologist* 32 (4):246–54. doi: 10.1037/0003-066X.32.4.246.

Nair, M. S., and R. Salleh. 2015. "Linking Performance Appraisal Justice, Trust, and Employee Engagement: A Conceptual Framework." *Procedia-Social and Behavioral Sciences* 211:1155–62. doi: 10.1016/j.sbspro.2015.11.154.

Pearce, J. L., I. Branyiczki, and G. A. Bigley. 2000. "Insufficient Bureaucracy: Trust and Commitment in Particularistic Organizations." *Organization Science* 11:148–62. doi: 10.1287/orsc.11.2.148.12508.

Podsakoff, P. M., S. B. MacKenzie, J.-Y. Lee, and N. P. Podsakoff. 2003. "Common Method Biases in Behavioral Research: A Critical Review of the Literature and Recommended Remedies." *Journal of Applied Psychology* 88 (5):879–903. doi: 10.1037/0021-9010.88.5.879.

Purcell, J., N. Kinnie, S. Hutchinson, B. Rayton, and J. Swart. 2003. *Understanding the People and Performance Link: Unlocking the Black Box.* London: Chartered Institute of Personnel and Development.

Robinson, S. L. 1996. "Trust and Breach of the Psychological Contract." *Administrative Science Quarterly* 41 (4): 574–99. doi: 10.2307/2393868.

Robinson, R. B., and J. A. Pearce. 1988. "Planned Patterns of Strategic Behaviour and their Relationship to Business-Unit Performance." *Strategic Management Journal* 9 (1):43–60. doi: 10.1002/smj.4250090105.

Rousseau, D. M., S. B. Sitkin, R. S. Burt, and C. F. Camerer. 1998. "Introduction to Special Topic Forum: Not so Different After All: A Cross-Discipline View of Trust." *Academy of Management Review* 23 (3):393–404. doi: 10.5465/amr.1998.926617.

Rousseau, D. M., and S. A. Tijoriwala. 1999. "What's a Good Reason to Change? Motivated Reasoning and Social Accounts in Promoting Organizational Change." *Journal of Applied Psychology* 84:514–28. doi: 10.1037/0021-9010.84.4.514.

Salamon-Deutsch, S. D., and S. L. Robinson. 2008. "Trust That Binds: The Impact of Collective Felt Trust on Organizational Performance." *Journal of Applied Psychology* 93 (3):593–601. doi: 10.1037/0021-9010.93.3.593.

Schneider, B., P. J. Hanges, D. Brent Smith, and N. Salvaggio. 2003. "Which Comes First: Employee Attitudes or Organizational Financial and Market Performance?" *Journal of Applied Psychology* 88 (5):836–51. Doi 10.1037/ 0021-9010.88.5.836

Searle, R., and G. Dietz. 2012. "Trust and HRM: Current Insights and Future Directions." *Human Resource Management Journal* 22 (4):333–42.

Spreitzer, G. M., and A. K. Mishra. 1999. "Giving Up Control without Losing Control: Trust and Its Substitutes' Effects on Managers' Involving Employees in Decision Making." *Group Organization Management* 24 (2): 155–87. doi: 10.1177/1059601199242003.

Tsui, A., J. Pearce, L. Porter, and A. Tripoli. 1997. "Alternative Approaches to the Employee-Organization Relationship: Does Investment in Employees Pay Off?" *Academy of Management Journal* 40 (5):1089–121. doi: 10.2307/256928.

Tsui, A., and J. Wu. 2005. "The New Employment Relationship Versus the Mutual Investment Approach: Implications for Human Resource Management." *Human Resource Management* 44 (2):115–21. doi: 10.1002/ hrm.20052.

Tzafrir, S. S. 2005. "The Relationship between Trust, HRM Practices and Firm Performance." *International Journal of Human Resource Management* 16 (9):1600–22. doi: 10.1080/09585190500239135.

Tzafrir, S. S., G. H. Harel, Y. Baruch, and S. Dolan. 2004. "The Consequences of Emerging HRM Practices for Employees' Trust in their Managers." *Personnel Review* 33 (6):628–47. doi: 10.1108/00483480410561529.

Ugwu, F. O., I. E. Onyishi, and A. M. Rodríguez-Sánchez. 2014. "Linking Organizational Trust with Employee Engagement: The Role of Psychological Empowerment." *Personnel Review* 43 (3):377–400. doi: 10.1108/PR-11-2012-0198.

Vanhala, M., and G. Dietz. 2015. "HRM, Trust in Employer and Organizational Performance." *Knowledge and Process Management* 22 (4):270–87. doi: 10.1002/kpm.1491.

Vanhala, M., K. Puumalainen, and K. Blomqvist. 2011. "Impersonal Trust – the Development of the Construct and the Scale." *Personnel Review* 40 (4):485–513. doi: 10.1108/00483481111133354.

Vanhala, M., and P. Ritala. 2016. "HRM Practices, Impersonal Trust and Organizational Innovativeness." *Journal of Managerial Psychology* 31 (1):95–109. doi: 10.1108/JMP-03-2013-0084.

Wall, T. D., and S. J. Wood. 2005. "The Romance of Human Resource Management and Business Performance and the Case for Big Science." *Human Relations* 58 (4):429–62. doi: 10.1177/0018726705055032.

Wat, D., and M. A. Shaffer. 2005. "Equity and Relationship Quality Influences on Organizational Citizenship Behaviors: The Mediating Role of Trust in the Supervisor and Empowerment." *Personnel Review* 34 (4):406–22. doi: 10.1108/00483480510599752.

Whitener, E. 1997. "The Impact of Human Resource Activities on Employee Trust." *Human Resource Management Review* 7 (4):389–404. doi: 10.1016/S1053-4822(97)90026-7.

Whitener, E. 2001. "Do 'High Commitment' Human Resource Practices Affect Employee Commitment? A Cross-Level Analysis Using Hierarchical Linear Modelling." *Journal of Management* 27:515–35. doi: 10.1177/ 014920630102700502.

Wright, P. M., T. M. Gardner, and L. M. Moynihan. 2003. "The Impact of HR Practices on the Performance of Business Units." *Human Resource Management Journal* 13 (3):21–36. doi: 10.1111/j.1748-8583.2003.tb00096.x.

Zeffane, R., and J. Connell. 2003. "Trust and HRM in the New Millennium." *International Journal of Human Resource Management* 14 (1):3–11. doi: 10.1080/09585190210158484.

APPENDIX 1:
Measurement items

	CONCEPT	ITEM	MEAN	SD	FACTOR LOADING	CR	α
HRM PRACTICES	LEARNING AND DEVELOPMENT	Learning (on the job) and training are encouraged in my organization.	3,30	1,02	.837a	.86	.86
		Employees are offered opportunities to develop their skills in order to help them advance in their careers.	3,12	1,02	.878***		
		Employees are encouraged to develop themselves and to learn new skills even if they are not directly related to their current position.	2,91	1,02	.737***		
	COMMUNICATION	Information on our business situation and plans is regularly provided to all employees.	2,90	1,01	.685a	.73	.73
		Information on our organization's financial results is provided to all employees.	3,39	1,01	.726***		
		The unit's performance targets are shared among all employees.	3,79	,94	.658***		
	PERFORMANCE EVALUTION AND REWARDS	Performance is evaluated by objective means.	2,86	,96	.775a	.69	.69
		Performance evaluation emphasize results.	3,35	,90	.599***		
		Performance evaluation include how results are achieved.	3,02	,77	.575***		
	CAREER OPPORTUNITIES	Individuals in my organization have the opportunity to develop and move to new tasks.	2,97	1,06	.757a	.52	.47
		Employees have very little future within this organization. (R)	2,79	1,06	.267***		
		Managers are aware of their subordinates' career aspirations.	3,13	,97	.483***		
	PARTICIPATION	Employees in my organization can participate in the decision-making.	2,50	,94	.807 [a]	.82	.81
		Employees are often asked by their managers to participate in the decision-making.	2,45	1,02	.805***		
		Employees are encouraged to suggest improvements in the way we work.	3,23	1,01	.716 ***		
	JOB DESIGN	We have flexible jobs and roles in my organization.	3,26	,98	.592a	.75	.74
		In my organization job rotation is in active use as a competence-development activity.	3,01	,93	.746***		
		In my organization jobs are deliberately allocated so as to exploit the employees'	3,03	,99	0,772***		

(Continued)

APPENDIX 1:
(Continued).

CONCEPT	ITEM	MEAN	SD	FACTOR LOADING	CR	α
	skills and abilities as effectively as possible.					
UNIT-LEVEL PERFORMANCE	My unit has been successful in advancing and supporting new business opportunities.	3.70	.901	.659 [a]	.75	.75
	My unit has prepared well for future opportunities and challenges.	3.55	.952	.695***		
	My unit has the relevant scientific, technical and professional knowledge to cope with future needs.	3.87	.887	.661***		
	My unit has adequate people and skills to convert ideas into new products and services, and to produce and implement them.	3.62	.974	.608***		
TRUST IN ORGANIZATION	There are work practices in my organization that help us to overcome exceptional situations.	3.35	.890	.598 [a]	.78	.78
	Employees have a bright future when working with this employer.	2.43	1.05	.617***		
	Our top management has a clear vision of the future.	3.17	1.198	.674***		
	I receive assistance with technical problems whenever I need it.	3.82	.933	.554***		
	Outsiders consider my employer to be a successful player in its field.	3.52	.941	.645***		
	The top management never puts their success ahead of that of the employees.	2.281	.966	.521***		
	Top management has made it clear that unethical action is not tolerated in my organization.	3.526	.950	.457***		

Measurement model (HRM practices and Unit-level performance): Chi-square = 445.16, df = 188, $p = 0.00$, RMSEA = 0.058, GFI = 0.910, NNFI = 0.973, CFI = 0.978, IFI = 0.978.

Measurement model (Trust in organization): Chi-square = 27.84, df = 14, $p = 0.015$, RMSEA = 0.049, GFI = 0.981, NNFI = 0.978, CFI = 0.985, IFI = 0.985.

[a]Significance level is not available, because the coefficient is fixed at 1.

***Statistically significant at 0.01 significance level.

Effect of Team-Member Exchange on Turnover Intention: A Cross-Cultural Perspective on a Selected Aspect of Employee Engagement

Lea Rutishauser (iD) and Anna Sender (iD)

Abstract: Research indicates that engaged employees demonstrate higher job satisfaction and lower turnover intention. However, employee engagement itself is influenced by and consists of a number of different factors. This study focuses on one specific aspect of employee engagement: the social interaction of team-members (i.e., team-member exchange, TMX) as a source of employee engagement. Drawing on social exchange theory, social information processing theory, and engagement literature, we investigate the role of societal culture on TMX, and we argue that the negative relationship of TMX and turnover intention is stronger in cultures high in collectivism and high in power distance. We combined the individual-level data of 6,664 employees from 14 countries with country-level data regarding the cultural values collectivism and power distance. Multilevel analysis supported the hypothesis that culture moderates the relationship between TMX and turnover intention such that the effect was stronger in cultures high in collectivism. However, power distance did not moderate the relationship between TMX and turnover intention. This study contributes to the research field by adding a cross-cultural perspective and testing country-level moderation effects. The practical implications of our findings are discussed.

INTRODUCTION

Social exchange relationships, such as relationships of employees with supervisors, team members, or organizations (Cropanzano and Mitchell 2005), constitute important resources which facilitate employee engagement (Liao et al. 2013; Saks 2006; Schaufeli and Bakker 2004) and thus employee attitudes and behaviors (Banks et al. 2014; Chiaburu and Harrison 2008; Cropanzano and Mitchell 2005; Farmer, van Dyne, and Kamdar 2015; Ng and Sorensen 2008). A collection of different topics, all having the purpose to keep employees engaged at work, constitutes the concept of employee engagement (Saks 2006). One of such topics is interpersonal relationships, which is in the focus of this research study. In addition to the extensively studied interpersonal relationship of employees with their organization and their supervisor, the less explored relationship between employees and their team (i.e., team-member exchange, TMX)−defined as "exchange quality with other team members, not as unique individuals, but in their shared role as team members" (Banks et al. 2014, 275)−positively influences job satisfaction, organizational commitment, job performance (Banks et al. 2014), and organizational citizenship behavior (Brandes, Dharwadkar, and Wheatley 2004; Chiaburu and Harrison 2008; Farmer et al. 2015), and negatively influences turnover intention (Banks et al. 2014).

Although TMX has been identified as antecedent of engagement, contributing to salient attitudinal and behavioral outcomes in general (Liao et al. 2013), less is known on how the aspect of social interactions with team members influence employees' attitudes across cultures. Several studies show that social exchange relationships and social networks may be influenced by culture (Dulebohn et al. 2012; Jung and Takeuchi 2014; Kim, Lee, and Lee 2013; Rockstuhl et al. 2012; Steiner 1988). However, given the limited empirical cross-cultural research on social relationships at work, scholars consequently called for consideration of the environmental (national) context in social exchange research (Coyle-Shapiro and Shore 2007; Hayton, Carnabuci, and Eisenberger 2012). From a cross-cultural perspective, such knowledge could help to identify cultures where the effects of TMX on salient outcomes such as engagement and turnover intention is most relevant (Schaufeli and Bakker 2004). In this study, we focus on the relationship of TMX on turnover intention to increase understanding the function of TMX in a multi-national setting. Thereby, we shed light on one specific aspect forming employee engagement and on the effect that cultural values may have on interpersonal relationships and its effect on employee turnover intention.

This study therefore investigates the moderating role of two cultural dimensions, collectivism and power distance, in the relationship between individually perceived TMX and employee turnover intention. We contribute to the current literature in three ways. First, whereas previously the relationships of employees with their supervisor and of employees with their organization have received attention for predicting employee engagement and job attitudes and behavior, we contribute by focusing on the still relatively underrepresented research about the relationship of employees with their teams (Farmer et al. 2015).

Secondly, we enrich current literature by investigating the moderating influence of situational factors (Banks et al. 2014; Cole, Schaninger, and Harris 2002; Dulebohn et al. 2012; Frenkel and Sanders 2007; Holtom et al. 2008), specifically the role of societal culture in the relationship between TMX and turnover intention. To date, research studies into social relations and employee turnover mainly took place in single-countries (Dulebohn et al. 2012) and in an Anglo-American context (e.g., Felps et al. 2009; Mitchell et al. 2001; Mossholder, Settoon, and Henagan 2005). However, no research addressed TMX and employee behavior in a broader cross-cultural context.

Our third contribution is of a methodological nature. Cross-cultural studies on social exchange relationships have mostly compared two countries (e.g., Jung and Takeuchi 2014; Kim et al. 2013; Ramesh and Gelfand 2010). However, to explain the effects of cultural values, it is important to include many cultures in the analysis simultaneously (van de Vijver and Leung 1997). We use a unique data set taken from 6,664 employees from 14 countries to test proposed hypotheses.

TMX AND TURNOVER INTENTION

Relationships that employees maintain within the organizational environment—such as with coworkers—complement the range of factors influencing retention management and employee turnover (Chiaburu and Harrison 2008; Holtom et al. 2008). Individuals have only limited time and resources to invest in social exchange relationships (Law, Wang, and Hui 2010; Shore et al. 2009). Thus, in line with social exchange theory (Blau 1964) and norm of reciprocity (Gouldner 1960), individuals develop social exchange relationships of a different quality in the workplace. Low quality exchange relationships are usually characterized by no further exchange than the role requirements of being an employee or peer (Nishii and Mayer 2009; Steiner 1988) or the work task requirement (Tse and Dasborough 2008). Thus, in low quality exchange relationships, social exchange is limited to task-related support. Consequently, employees and their colleagues interact and thus engage less compared to employees with high quality relationships that go beyond what is required by the work task (Tse and Dasborough 2008).

Literature suggests that TMX has several mechanisms, which could affect employees' turnover intention. First, in line with engagement literature, high quality TMX may influence employee engagement, and thus may impact employee attitudes and behavior through three factors (Kahn 1990; May, Gilson, and Harter 2004): psychological safety ("feeling able to show and employ one's self without fear of negative consequences to self-image, status, or career"; [Kahn 1990, 708]), meaningfulness ("a feeling that one is receiving a return on investments of one's self in a currency of physical, cognitive, or emotional energy"; [Kahn 1990, 703–704]), and availability ("the sense of having the physical, emotional, or psychological resources to personally engage at a particular moment"; [Kahn 1990, 714]). High quality TMX may fulfill employees' need for relatedness (meaningsfulness) and it may constitute a source of support and lack of threat (psychological safety). As a result, engaged employees may demonstrate lower turnover intention in the workplace.

Secondly, in line with social exchange theory and norm of reciprocity, employees who receive social support from their network in the organization will reciprocate in the form of organizational commitment (Ng and Sorensen 2008) and lower turnover intention (Chiaburu and Harrison 2008; Holtom et al. 2008; Ng and Sorensen 2008). Employees perceive peers and supervisors as part of the network in the organization, which constitutes organizational support (Hayton et al. 2012; Kalemci Tuzun and Arzu Kalemci 2012). Consequently, employees develop feelings of belongingness and emotional bonds with and attachment to the organization (Farmer et al. 2015; Frenkel and Sanders 2007; Mossholder et al. 2005).

Thirdly, embeddedness literature suggests that the threat of losing the good conditions of the work environment (e.g., high quality social exchange relationships) is a likely reason for reduced turnover intention. An employee who leaves a workplace with a high level of TMX would sacrifice a lot (Mitchell et al. 2001; Ramesh and Gelfand 2010), because such relationships are not easily replaced at a new employer's. Consequently, leaving the organization may be harder for employees who have more to lose in terms of relationships with their team.

In sum, social exchange perspective, job engagement, and job embeddedness literature suggest that high quality TMX leads to support from and attachment to the organization (Frenkel and Sanders 2007) and lower turnover intention. Empirical studies have demonstrated that TMX decreases individuals' turnover intention accordingly (e.g., Banks et al. 2014; Holtom et al. 2008; Ng and Sorensen 2008). Thus, as a basic relationship we propose the following hypothesis:

Hypothesis 1. There is a negative relationship between TMX and turnover intention.

INTEGRATING SOCIAL INFORMATION PROCESSING THEORY AND SOCIETAL CULTURE

The relationship between TMX and turnover intention is likely to vary with situational factors such as societal culture. By definition, societal culture provides a set of "shared motives, values, beliefs, identities, and interpretations of meanings of significant events that result from common experience of members of collectives that are transmitted across generations" (House et al. 2004, 15). Social information processing theory (Salancik and Pfeffer 1978) posits that situational context influences an individual's reception, perception, and reflection, as well as the handling of information. As Salancik and Pfeffer (1978, 226) indicated ". . . the definition of the relationship between an individual and the environment takes place in a social context and is influenced by that context."

Given that societal culture is a situational context, according to social processing theory (Salancik and Pfeffer 1978), it is likely to influence the perceptions of individuals about attitudes, behavior, and roles within a society. The observation of peer groups allows individuals to derive norms (Morris and Liu 2015). Specifically, the social environment provides an important source of information (e.g., what a person's attitudes and behavior should be) and offers strategies on how to interpret events (Salancik and Pfeffer 1978). Consequently, individuals tend to adjust their attitude and beliefs to the social environment they are in. Thus, as a result of such social information processing, people develop shared perceptions. These perceptions relate, amongst others, to appropriate attitudes and needs, definitions of work and environment, and how people should relate to that environment (Salancik and Pfeffer 1978). Adherence to norms enables individuals to build relationships and establish power (Morris and Liu 2015). Consequently, individuals in a given culture form a shared understanding of how interpersonal relationships in the workplace should look. Thus, culture likely provides individuals with a common conceptualization of the role and behavior of employees in teams.

Previous studies suggest that culture comprises different dimensions (e.g., Hofstede 2001; House et al. 2004; Taras, Rowney, and Steel 2009; Triandis 2001). For this study−examining the influence of TMX on turnover intention across cultures−we chose to focus on the two cultural dimensions of collectivism and power distance. We selected these two cultural dimensions because they best describe the relationships people have with each other (Dickson et al. 2012; Taras et al. 2009; Tsui, Nifadkar, and Ou 2007), they have been widely used in comparative studies (Tsui et al. 2007), and are thus suitable in exploring the role of culture in the context of TMX.

Collectivism is characterized by the "extent to which people are autonomous individuals or embedded in their groups" (House et al. 2004, 440). In cultures low in collectivism freedom, both autonomy and independency from groups are important. The focus is on achieving individual goals rather than group goals. In cultures high in collectivism, individuals are perceived as being part of a societal context. The society values interdependent relationships and favoring the group over the self.

Power distance refers to the relationship that employees maintain with others from different levels of power within an organization (e.g., exchange relationship with supervisor and peers). Specifically, power distance is characterized by the way people perceive hierarchy between individuals (Hofstede 1980). According to the concept of power distance, a society or organization is divided into different levels of power. The extent to which individuals from a lower level of power accept the unequal power distribution, determines the level of power distance in a society (Hofstede 1980; House et al. 2004). In brief, power distance is high if a society accepts the inequality of power distribution. If this inequality is not accepted, power distance is low.

INTERACTIVE EFFECTS OF TMX AND COLLECTIVISM

We argue that both the cultural dimensions of collectivism and power distance influence the role of TMX in terms of turnover intention. Specifically, the level of a society's collectivism and power distance provides a social context, which leads–in line with social information processing theory–to assumptions which are implicit about the characteristics of TMX relationships. Thus, our study is characterized as a type II study, which considers culture as a moderating factor (Tsui et al. 2007). We argue that in cultures high in collectivism, the relationship between TMX and turnover intention will be stronger, compared to cultures low in collectivism.

In cultures low in collectivism, employees engage mainly in task-related peer support (Farh, Zhong, and Organ 2004) and consider the decision whether to provide any support at all and to whom as a personal choice (Perlow and Weeks 2002). In cultures low in collectivism, social environment emphasizes and values autonomy, independency from groups, and prioritization of self-interest (House et al. 2004). According to Perlow and Weeks (2002), employees in cultures low in collectivism primarily engage in supporting behavior with peers from whom they expect support in the future (reciprocity).

In cultures high in collectivism, employees engage in interactions with others, mutual exchange, and support (House et al. 2004). Contrary to low collectivistic cultures, providing support is not a personal choice but a moral responsibility (Perlow and Weeks 2002). Supporting others is an obligation and highly valued by society members (Perlow and

Weeks 2002). Consequently, we argue that in cultures high in collectivism, employees receive more TMX and value it more strongly. Empirical research supports this notion. For example, Ramesh and Gelfand (2010) showed that in collectivistic India the relationship between links employees have in the organization and actual turnover is stronger than in the individualistic United States. In sum, we hypothesize that in collectivistic countries, high TMX has a higher importance for employees in terms of their turnover intention.

Hypothesis 2. The cultural dimension of collectivism moderates the negative relationship between TMX and turnover intention, such that the relationship is stronger in cultures high in collectivism.

INTERACTIVE EFFECTS OF TMX AND POWER DISTANCE

Power distance influences team related factors such as the hierarchical structure of the work environment, the support, proximity, and communication between employees and individuals higher in the hierarchy. Distance between superiors and employees in high power distance work settings could strengthen the bonds that employees have with their peers and with their team in the same or a similar situation (Hauff and Richter 2015; Ng and Sorensen 2008). Where power distance is high, employees have the impression that people higher in the hierarchy (e.g., supervisor or management) have a lot more power than they themselves have (Steiner 1988). This creates dependency of the employee on their supervisor and other individuals higher in the hierarchy (Hauff and Richter 2015, House et al. 2004). Employees will therefore have less direct and less open communication with superiors (Hauff and Richter 2015). In low power distance cultures, both flat hierarchies and proximity between employees and authorities allow employees to approach supervisors or management with their concerns directly.

The processing of social information from the cultural environment of high power distance leads to implicit assumptions about the characteristic of relationships between employees and their team. In high power distance cultures, TMX is important for employees in order to compensate for the hierarchical distance to the authorities and make the relationships between employees more important (Hauff and Richter 2015). Consequently, in cultures with high power distance, the impact of TMX on employee engagement (via greater psychological safety and meaningfulness, which are less available from the supervisor in this situation) will thus lead to a stronger effect on turnover intention. However, the small amount of empirical research on the role of power distance on the effect of relationships with the team is not conclusive. For example, Hauff and Richter (2015) investigated whether power distance moderates the connection between relationships with colleagues and job satisfaction and found no significant moderation effects.

One might argue that power distance is important for leadership, but less so for team processes. However, as the hierachical structure of an organization also impacts the degree of self-organization of a team and the influence a leader exerts (Burt 2005), power distance is likely to influence the TMX relationship. Guided by the information processing theory, we propose as follows:

Hypothesis 3. The cultural dimension of power distance moderates the negative relationship between TMX and turnover intention, such that the relationship is stronger in cultures high in power distance.

METHODS

Sample and Procedure

To observe the cross-cultural effects on the relationship between TMX relations and turnover intention, we link data from employees from 14 countries with their respective cultural values. Table 1 lists the countries included in this study and the values of the cultural dimension collectivism and power distance (according to GLOBE 2016; House et al. 2004), as well as the countries' group size.

Individual-level data for this study are derived from the annual survey on diverse organizations involving 29 countries, conducted by a leading market research institute. We only included data from individuals who were employees and did not have a manager-function. Additionally, given that individuals who are working for multinational companies may be exposed to organizational cultures conflicting with societal culture, and given that we only

TABLE 1.
Size, Cultural Values, and Unemployment Rate Per Country

Countries	Group size	In-Group Collectivism		Power Distance		Unemployment rate (%)
		Value	*Band*	*Value*	*Band*	
Austria	364	4.85	B	4.95	B	4.6
Brazil	371	5.18	B	5.33	A	6.7
Canada	680	4.26	C	4.82	B	7.5
Colombia	251	5.73	A	5.56	A	10.8
Hungary	440	5.25	B	5.56	A	11
Mexico	184	5.71	A	5.22	B	5.2
Netherlands	406	3.7	C	4.11	D	4.4
Philippines	130	6.36	A	5.44	A	7
Poland	443	5.52	A	5.1	B	9.6
Portugal	326	5.51	A	5.44	A	12.7
Russia	342	5.63	A	5.52	A	6.5
Turkey	285	5.88	A	5.57	A	8.8
UK	356	4.08	C	5.15	B	8
US	2086	4.25	C	4.88	B	9

Average group size = 476; Values indicate the aggregated individual answers on country level. Bands indicate clusters of countries with non-significant variance within the bands but significant variance between the bands. Unemployment rate in % of unemployed people out of the total number of employed and unemployed persons in a country.

investigated societal culture in this study, we excluded participants whose employers were present in more than one country.

Country-level data for power distance and collectivism are derived from the GLOBE study (GLOBE 2016; House et al. 2004)—a research project about leadership and organizational practices involving 62 countries. Combining the two data sets, 14 countries were a match, (Austria, Brazil, Canada, Colombia, Hungary, Mexico, Netherlands, Philippines, Poland, Portugal, Russia, Turkey, United Kingdom, and the United States), resulting in a sample of 6,664 participants (see Table 1).

Measures

Individual-Level Variables

All individual-level data was measured with a 5-point Likert scale ranging from strongly disagree (=1) to strongly agree (=5).

TMX Despite its advantages, the dataset used in this study limits the measurements to available items. Therefore, we used a non-validated measure of perceived TMX. Specifically, we used the following three items: "In our team, I can rely on support from my colleagues when I need it," "In our team, we all respect and value each other," and "In our team, we all take responsibility for achieving our teams' key goals." These items correspond to items used in the TMX measure of Seers (1989) such as support (e.g., "others help me learn better work methods"), respect (e.g., "other members recognize my potential"), and commitment to team goals (e.g., "how willing others are to finish work assigned to me"). The three items of the TMX scale all loaded on one factor and achieved an acceptable reliability level of coefficient alpha 0.87. Moreover, confirmatory factor analysis of all three items together showed a good fit ($\chi^2=120.321$; $df=16$; CFI = 0.995; RMSEA = 0.032; SRMR = 0.009).

Turnover Intention Turnover intention was measured with one item, "Are you currently looking for a new job?" Although using a single-item is not ideal for measuring turnover intention, previous studies proceeded the same way (e.g., Grover and Crooker 1995; Harris, Kacmar, and Witt 2005).

Country-Level Variables

The cultural values of collectivism and power distance were operationalized using the in-group collectivism scores and the power distance scores from the GLOBE study (GLOBE 2016; House et al. 2004). In line with previous research (Atwater et al. 2009; Debus et al. 2012; Sturman, Shao, and Katz 2012), we used scores of societal practices ("as is") not societal values ("should be"). Societal practices capture perceptions concerning current practices in societies, whereas societal values reveal the values with respect to what the respondents wish would be practiced in the society (House et al. 2004). We chose to use societal practices because they most likely reflect the ways values are currently practiced and therefore may directly influence interpersonal interactions in each culture (Atwater et al. 2009). In the GLOBE study, researchers aggregated participants' responses on a country-level and clustered them onto bands (House et al. 2004). Given that bands indicate clusters of countries with non-significant within-group variance, but with significant between-group variance, we use these bands for clustering the countries in the analysis (House et al. 2004).

Collectivism In-group collectivism practices scores from the GLOBE study (4 items) measured individuals' feelings of pride, cohesiveness, and loyalty in their organization and/or family (House et al. 2004). Given that in our sample we had a relatively high number of countries with a high level of collectivism (Band A; see Table 1), we created a dummy variable for high collectivistic culture (1 = countries with values in Band A; 0 = countries with values in Band B and C; see Table 1).

Power Distance Power distance practices scores from the GLOBE study (4 items) measured individuals' expectations and agreement on how power should be distributed in society (House et al. 2004). Given that in our sample we have employees from many countries in Band A and B and only one country in Band D, we created a dummy variable for high power distance culture (1 = countries, with values in Band A, 0 = countries with values in Band B until D; see Table 1).

Control Variables

Given that national samples differ in terms of demographic variables and that demographic variables have been found to relate to turnover (Griffeth, Hom, and Gaertner 2000), we included a number of control variables (Tsui et al. 2007) which may influence turnover intention on an individual-level: Age, gender (0 = female, 1 = male), and tenure. Age and tenure were measured as aforementioned in ranges rather than actual values. Age was measured with 10 categories (1 = 18–24 years, 2–9 = 5 year steps e.g., 25–29 years, 30–34 years etc., 10 = older than 65 years). Tenure was measured with 5 categories (1 = less than 1 year, 2 = 1–2 years, 3 = 2–5 years, 4 = 5–10 years, 5 = more than 10 years).

Furthermore, we added job satisfaction, perceived employability, and organizational size to the control variables, known as antecedents of turnover intention (e.g., Hulin, Roznowski, and Hachiya 1985). Job satisfaction was measured with one item, "Thinking of your personal work situation, how satisfied are you with your job?" on a 5-point Likert scale (1 = very dissatisfied, 5 = very satisfied). Perceived employability was measured with one item, "I feel there are still plenty of job opportunities available for me on the market" on a 5-point Likert scale (1 = strongly disagree, 5 = strongly agree). As effects of TMX may differ in an environment with a small number of employees compared to an environment with several hundreds or thousands of employees, we controlled for organizational size (0 = small and medium size organizations with <250 employees, 1 = big size organizations with 250 or more employees; OECD 2005).

In addition to individual level variables, we also controlled for the unemployment rate at the time of the survey (International Labour Organization 2016). In 2011, some countries were still struggling with the effects of economic downturn and its consequences on the labor market. Scholars have indicated that contextual factors other than culture could provide alternative explanations to differences observed across nations (Tsui et al. 2007). The unemployment rate for our sample ranged from 4.4% (Netherlands) to 12.7% (Portugal).

ANALYSIS

As our data set consisted of two data levels (Level 1 = individuals, Level 2 = countries), we used hierarchical linear modeling to capture the nested structure of the individuals' societal culture (Tsui et al. 2007).

To test the hypotheses, we followed a hierarchical test procedure of Aguinis, Gottfredson, and Culpepper (2013) and conducted the analysis in four steps, each consisting of a model (see Table 3). Model 1 included the unconditional model (null model) in order to estimate the total systemic variance in the outcome variable. We then entered control variables, the main effect, and the moderators into Model 2 and calculated the random intercept and fixed slope model. For Model 3, we ran random intercept and random slope models, and in Model 4 and Model 5, we included interaction terms of TMX with collectivism and with power distance, respectively. To compare the nested models, parameters were estimated using full information maximum likelihood (FIML).

RESULTS

Descriptive Statistics

Table 2 presents the means, standard deviations, and correlations of all variables included in the analysis. In line with previous research, TMX ($r = -0.33$, $p < 0.01$) is negatively correlated with turnover intention.

We calculated the intra-class correlation (ICC) to examine within- and between-group variance in turnover intention. The variance explained by the higher-level data is 8.2%. If the ICC is sufficiently close to zero, no multilevel modeling is necessary (Hayes 2006). However, no cutoff value, that would define an ICC as being sufficiently close to zero, exists. Muthen (1999) draws on a study about design effects from Muthen and Satorra (1995) and suggests that design effects > 2 indicate that clustering in the data needs to be considered. She defines the design effect as follows:

$$1 + (average\ cluster\ size - 1) * ICC$$

If we take the average cluster size of our sample (=476, see Table 1) into account, we reach a design effect size where Muthen (1999) strongly recommends using multilevel modeling.

TABLE 2.
Means, Standard Deviations (SD), and Correlations

Variable	Mean	SD	1)	2)	3)	4)	5)	6)	7)	8)	9)	10)	11)
1) Collectivism	0.29	0.46	—	0.43	0.36	-0.73**	-0.69**	0.49	-0.79**	0.41	-0.37	0.28	0.55*
2) Power distance	0.32	0.47	0.50**	—	0.27	-0.61*	-0.56*	0.21	-0.54*	0.22	-0.51	0.45	0.48
3) TMX	3.77	0.90	0.03*	0.01	—	-0.20	-0.15	-0.14	-0.35	0.26	0.30	-0.02	-0.07
4) Age	5.72	2.45	-0.37**	-0.34**	0.01	—	0.82**	-0.58*	0.53	-0.62*	0.56*	0.05	-0.73**
5) Tenure	3.36	1.57	-0.20**	-0.18**	-0.02	0.40**	—	-0.51	0.35	-0.75**	0.68**	0.02	-0.83**
6) Gender	0.41	0.49	0.13**	0.10**	-0.02	-0.03*	-0.02	—	-0.43	0.16	-0.37	0.19	0.34
7) Organizational size	0.41	0.49	-0.14**	-0.10**	-0.01	0.07**	0.17**	0.00	—	0.01	0.17	-0.57*	-0.22
8) Employability	3.08	1.18	0.16**	0.10**	0.15**	-0.26**	-0.16**	0.09**	0.00	—	-0.19	-0.52	0.52
9) Job satisfaction	3.73	1.00	-0.07**	-0.11**	0.50**	0.10**	0.05**	-0.05**	0.00	0.12**	—	-0.16	-0.81**
10) Unemployment rate	8.28	2.07	0.23**	0.32**	0.00	0.08**	0.01	0.02	-0.09**	-0.22**	-0.02*	—	0.00
11) Turnover intention	1.95	1.25	0.17**	0.16**	-0.33**	-0.23**	-0.23**	0.06**	-0.08**	0.07**	-0.53**	-0.01	—

Correlations below the diagonal are individual-level correlations ($N = 6,664$). Correlations above the diagonal are country-level correlations, with individual-level measures aggregated to the country-level ($N = 14$). Collectivism: $1 =$ high collectivism, $0 =$ else; Power distance: $1 =$ high power distance, $0 =$ else; Gender: $1 =$ male, $0 =$ female; Organizational size: $1 = 250$ or more employees, $0 =$ less than 250 employees.

$*p < 0.5$; $**p < 0.01$.

TABLE 3.
Results of Hierarchical Linear Regression for Turnover Intention

Variable	Model 1	Model 2	Model 3	Model 4	Model 5
Intercept	2.08*** (0.09)	1.96*** (0.17)	1.99*** (0.16)	1.95*** (0.12)	1.97*** (0.16)
Age		-0.03*** (0.01)	-0.04*** (0.01)	-0.04*** (0.01)	-0.04*** (0.01)
Tenure		-0.11*** (0.01)	-0.11*** (0.01)	-0.11*** (0.01)	-0.11*** (0.01)
Gender		0.04 (0.03)	0.05 (0.03)	0.05 (0.03)	0.05 (0.03)
Organizational Size		-0.12*** (0.03)	-0.12*** (0.03)	-0.11*** (0.03)	-0.12*** (0.03)
Employability		0.09*** (0.01)	0.09*** (0.01)	0.09*** (0.01)	0.09*** (0.01)
Job Satisfaction		-0.57*** (0.01)	-0.58*** (0.01)	-0.58*** (0.01)	-0.58*** (0.01)
Unemployment rate		-0.02 (0.02)	-0.01 (0.02)	-0.01 (0.02)	-0.01 (0.02)
TMX		-0.16*** (0.02)	-0.18*** (0.03)	-0.13*** (0.03)	-0.16*** (0.04)
Collectivism		0.13 (0.11)	0.04 (0.10)	0.12 (0.11)	0.04 (0.10)
Power distance		0.10 (0.12)	0.10 (0.11)	0.09 (0.11)	0.13 (0.11)
TMX x Collectivism				-0.12* (0.04)	
TMX x Power distance					-0.05 (0.05)
Variance components					
Within-country variance ($\sigma2$)	1.4409	0.97361	0.96865	0.96880	0.96873
Intercept (L2) variance ($\tau00$)	0.1283	0.03032	0.02964	0.02845	0.02958
Slope (L2) variance ($\tau11$)			0.00634	0.00272	0.00541
Intercept-slope (L2) covariance ($\tau01$)			-0.00767	-0.00537	-0.00734
$-2*\log(lh)$	21395.40	18769.00	18747.20	18741.87	18746.36
Diff-2*log		2626.40***	21.90***	5.33 *	0.84
Df	3	13	15	16	16
Pseudo R2		0.123	0.124	0.124	0.124

Estimates and standard errors (in parentheses).
FIML: full information maximum likelihood estimation.
*$p < 0.05$; **$p < 0.01$; ***$p < 0.001$.

Hierarchical Linear Modeling

Table 3 presents the results of the hierarchical linear modeling described in what follows. Results support Hypothesis 1 (Model 2). TMX relates negatively to turnover intention ($\gamma = -0.16$, $p < 0.001$). To test Hypothesis 2, we examined the moderating effect of collectivism on the relationship between TMX and turnover intention (Model 4). The interaction term of collectivism and TMX was significant ($\gamma = -0.12$, $p < 0.05$). Thus, Hypothesis 2 was supported. Additionally, Model 4 shows a significantly better fit than Model 3 ($\Delta\chi^2 = 5.33$, $\Delta df = 1$, $p < 0.05$). A simple slope test indicates that for low level of collectivism (collectivism = 0), the relationship between TMX and turnover intention is weaker ($\gamma = -0.13$, $p < 0.001$) than for high level of collectivism (collectivism = 1; $\gamma = -0.25$, $p < 0.001$). Figure 1 presents this effect graphically.

To test Hypothesis 3, we examined the moderating effect of power distance on the relationship between TMX and turnover intention (Model 5). The moderating effect of power distance on the relationship between TMX and turnover intention was not significant ($\gamma = -0.05$, $p > 0.10$). Thus Hypothesis 3 was not supported.

Explained with this multilevel approach, the overall variance in employees' turnover intention is 12.4% for the interaction between TMX and collectivism, showing a medium effect size.

DISCUSSION

The objective of the current study was to provide a cross-cultural perspective on the role of TMX. We found that the relationship between TMX and turnover intention was moderated by country-level variable collectivism. Specifically, we showed that, in cultures with higher

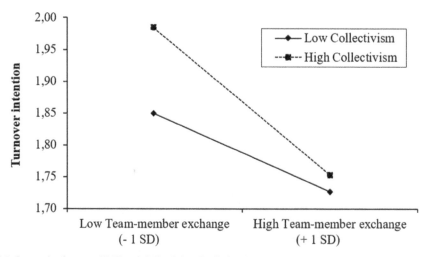

FIGURE 1. Interaction between TMX and Collectivism Predicting Turnover Intention

collectivism, the negative relationship between TMX and turnover intention was stronger than in countries low in collectivism. Using social processing theory (Salancik and Pfeffer 1978), we argued that in cultures high in collectivism, employees value TMX more than in cultures low in collectivism. Next we investigated the moderating effect of power distance. However, our results do not indicate support for our hypothesis that in countries with high power distance, the relationship between TMX and turnover intention is stronger than in countries low in power distance. Thus, our results corroborate previous studies which have argued for but have not found a significant interaction effect of power distance on the relation between relationships with colleagues and job attitudes (Hauff and Richter 2015).

Theoretical Implications

Our study contributes to the turnover and social exchange literature by showing that the strength of the relationship between TMX and turnover intention depends on cultural context. Firstly, we contribute to the understanding about the influence of social interaction in teams on employee turnover intention (Holtom et al. 2008; Regts and Molleman 2013). Although research has focused increasingly on the role of team level phenomena and social context in explaining employee turnover (e.g., Felps et al. 2009; Ramesh and Gelfand 2010), more work is needed in order to fully understand to what extent and in which circumstances relationships with teammates are salient predictors of turnover attitudes and behavior.

Secondly, we contribute to the social exchange literature. Although scholars have acknowledged that social exchange relationships in the workplace are embedded on different levels within an organization (e.g., Banks et al. 2014; Farh et al. 2004; Frenkel and Sanders 2007; Ng and Sorensen 2008), we demonstrate that country level variables (i.e., cultural values) provide an important context in which relationships operate. Specifically, we argued that cultural values may influence implicit assumptions about how a social exchange relationship should look and to what extent such relationships are valued in that society. Thus, results suggest that, depending on the cultural context, social exchange theory may be helpful in explaining why exchange between team members is fruitful in fostering positive job attitudes. By examining the moderating effect of cultural values in the TMX–turnover intention relationship, we addressed the recommendation of several researchers to include social environment variables in the research on social exchange relationships (Banks et al. 2014; Cole et al. 2002; Dulebohn et al. 2012; Frenkel and Sanders 2007; Holtom et al. 2008). Furthermore, this is one of the first studies that includes, not only one cultural value as a boundary condition, but both collectivism and power distance. We have therefore increased the understanding on when TMX is valuable to employees, not only from the perspective of collectivism (Ramesh and Gelfand 2010), but also from the power distance perspective, which has up till now been mostly explored in leadership literature (e.g., Dulebohn et al. 2012; Kirkman et al. 2009).

Our third contribution is of a methodological nature. Specifically, we combined a unique and rich dataset with data of the GLOBE study, to explore the role of country level cultural values in explaining individual level attitudes. We contribute to the current literature by investigating this individual level and country level data with a multilevel analysis and thereby explain additional variance in employees' turnover intention.

Practical Implications

Our results suggest that although some differences between cultures can be observed, TMX is a significant predictor of turnover intention across cultures. Given that organizations become flatter, greater attention should be devoted to horizontal peer relationships, such as teams (Banks et al. 2014). Social support among employees influences employee engagement (Schaufeli and Bakker 2004). Thus, our research indicates that irrespective of culture, the role of TMX is an important aspect to consider when designing retention programs. By emphasizing and supporting the development of social exchange relationships, it is possible that organizations could reduce turnover intention among workforce. Reduced turnover intention in an organization would lead to less actual employee turnover and thus, to a decrease in costs for replacements and an increase in benefits of social exchange in the workplace (e.g., by using existing networks for information and resources; Dess and Shaw 2001).

Moreover, turnover intention decreases with quality in TMX relationships, and this decrease is strongest under certain cultural conditions. Specifically, the relationship between TMX and turnover intention is stronger in cultures high in collectivism. Given that many organizations operate in multi-cultural contexts, managerial practices should consider this result. This study reveals that human resources management practices should be adapted to the cultural context. Although, regarding reducing turnover intention, TMX relationships are universally important, investing resources in order to develop high quality TMX relationships will achieve the best results in high collectivistic cultures.

There are multiple ways in which organizations can improve TMX among employees; one approach is for managers to create a work environment that promotes collaboration (Liu, Loi, and Lam 2011; Seers 1989). As TMX also contributes to employees' perception of organizational support, this is especially important in situations where the organization or the supervisor cannot provide the necessary support. One measure for creating more employee-team interaction would be to establish work spaces where teams spend time together, and where they also have the opportunity to exchange ideas beyond task-related topics that are necessary for work (Banks et al. 2014). Moreover, companies may consider organizing training opportunities for team members to develop the necessary competencies to engage in high-quality TMX relationships (Banks et al. 2014).

Limitations and Further Research

The strength of the current study lies in the use of a unique, large, international sample, and the integration of country-level variables. Even so, an obvious limitation is that the cultural values are only aggregated on the country-level and do not allow the individuals' value perceptions in those countries to be examined. Although we apply the recommended method in investigating cross-cultural data (van de Vijver and Leung 1997), future research should include data on individual culture perception so that the reliability of our findings is strengthened (Tsui et al. 2007).

Furthermore, the underlying data does not reveal participants' nationality, but only their country of work. However, as we use the societal practices rather than the societal values of the cultural values, we capture the perception of how the cultural values are in a country and not how they should be. Consequently, it is more relevant to do the analysis using participants' place of work rather than their nationality.

Moreover, replicas of this study—with different measures of TMX and culture—could strengthen the non-validated scales herein and are therefore encouraged. Another limitation relates to the fact that the samples differed, for example, in terms of age, tenure, or gender between countries. Thus, although we control for these factors, we are not able to assure sample equivalence in terms of demographics (Tsui et al. 2007).

Last, as TMX is one aspect of employee engagement, the findings of cultural influence on the TMX–turnover intention relationship lead to the assumption that societal culture may also have implications on employee engagement. Thus, further research should investigate the influence of cultures on employee engagement and on different topics related to and being part of the construct of employee engagement.

CONCLUSION

Considering the social environment of employees reveals that the effect on turnover intention depends on culture although TMX relationships are universally salient. By integrating social information processing theory, we have shed light on the role of culture for TMX relationships on employees' turnover intention and found a stronger impact in cultures high in collectivism but not in power distance. As teams and the exchange between employees and their teams are central for employee engagement and thus, for turnover intention, the findings of this study are important for theory and practice.

ACKNOWLEDGEMENTS

The authors thank GfK for providing the data used in this research project. The authors also thank EIASM for organizing the Workshop for Strategic Human Resource Management that provided the opportunity to engage in this discussion. We also thank the French Investissements d'Avenir (ANR-11-IDEX-0003/Labex Ecodec/ANR-11-LABX-0047) for funding the original working group for this special issue. Additionally, we thank HEC Paris School of Management and NEOMA Business School for their support of this project.

ORCID

Lea Rutishauser ⓘ http://orcid.org/0000-0002-0556-4687
Anna Sender ⓘ http://orcid.org/0000-0002-7013-7390

REFERENCES

Aguinis, H., R. K. Gottfredson, and S. A. Culpepper. 2013. "Best-Practice Recommendations for Estimating Cross-Level Interaction Effects Using Multilevel Modeling." *Journal of Management* 39 (6):1490–528. doi: 10.1177/0149206313478188.

Atwater, L., M. Wang, J. W. Smither, and J. W. Fleenor. 2009. "Are Cultural Characteristics Associated with the Relationship between Self and Others' Ratings of Leadership?" *Journal of Applied Psychology* 94 (4):876–86. doi: 10.1037/a0014561.

Banks, G. C., J. H. Batchelor, A. Seers, E. H. O'Boyle, J. M. Pollack, and K. Gower. 2014. "What Does Team–Member Exchange Bring to the Party? A Meta-Analytic Review of Team and Leader Social Exchange." *Journal of Organizational Behavior* 35 (2):273–95. doi: 10.1002/job.1885.

Blau, P. M. 1964. *Exchange and Power in Social Life.* New York: Wiley.

Brandes, P., R. Dharwadkar, and K. Wheatley. 2004. "Social Exchanges within Organizations and Work Outcomes: The Importance of Local and Global Relationships." *Group and Organization Management* 29 (3):276–301. doi: 10.1177/1059601103257405.

Burt, R. S. 2005. *Brokerage and Closure: An Introduction to Social Capital.* Oxford: Oxford University Press.

Chiaburu, D. S., and D. A. Harrison. 2008. "Do Peers Make the Place? Conceptual Synthesis and Meta-Analysis of Coworker Effects on Perceptions, Attitudes, OCBs, and Performance." *Journal of Applied Psychology* 93 (5):1082–103. doi: 10.1037/0021-9010.93.5.1082.

Cole, M. S., W. S. Schaninger, and S. G. Harris. 2002. "The Workplace Social Exchange Network: A Multilevel, Conceptual Examination." *Group and Organization Management* 27 (1):142–67. doi: 10.1177/1059601102027001008.

Coyle-Shapiro, J., and L. M. Shore. 2007. "The Employee–Organization Relationship: Where Do We Go from Here?" *Human Resource Management Review* 17 (2):166–79. doi: 10.1016/j.hrmr.2007.03.008.

Cropanzano, R., and M. S. Mitchell. 2005. "Social Exchange Theory: An Interdisciplinary Review." *Journal of Management* 31 (6):874–900. doi: 10.1177/0149206305279602.

Debus, M. E., T. M. Probst, C. J. König, and M. Kleinmann. 2012. "Catch Me If I Fall! Enacted Uncertainty Avoidance and the Social Safety Net as Country-Level Moderators in the Job Insecurity-Job Attitudes Link." *Journal of Applied Psychology* 97 (3):690–8. doi: 10.1037/a0027832.

Dess, G. G., and J. D. Shaw. 2001. "Voluntary Turnover, Social Capital, and Organizational Performance." *Academy of Management Review* 26 (3):446–56. doi: 10.5465/amr.2001.4845830.

Dickson, M. W., N. Castaño, A. Magomaeva, and D. N. Den Hartog. 2012. "Conceptualizing Leadership across Cultures." *Journal of World Business* 47 (4):483–92. doi: 10.1016/j.jwb.2012.01.002.

Dulebohn, J. H., W. H. Bommer, R. C. Liden, R. L. Brouer, and G. R. Ferris. 2012. "A Meta-Analysis of Antecedents and Consequences of Leader-Member Exchange Integrating the past with an Eye toward the Future." *Journal of Management* 38 (6):1715–59. doi: 10.1177/0149206311415280.

Farh, J.-L., C.-B. Zhong, and D. W. Organ. 2004. "Organizational Citizenship Behavior in the People's Republic of China." *Organization Science* 15 (2):241–53. doi: 10.1287/orsc.1030.0051.

Farmer, S. M., L. van Dyne, and D. Kamdar. 2015. "The Contextualized Self: How Team–Member Exchange Leads to Coworker Identification and Helping OCB." *Journal of Applied Psychology* 100 (2):583–95. doi: 10.1037/a0037660.

Felps, W., T. R. Mitchell, D. R. Hekman, T. W. Lee, B. C. Holtom, and W. S. Harman. 2009. "Turnover Contagion: How Coworkers' Job Embeddedness and Job Search Behaviors Influence Quitting." *Academy of Management Journal* 52 (3):545–61. doi: 10.5465/amj.2009.41331075.

Frenkel, S. J., and K. Sanders. 2007. "Explaining Variations in Co-Worker Assistance in Organizations." *Organization Studies* 28 (6):797–823. doi: 10.1177/0170840607073079.

GLOBE. 2016. "Understanding the Relationship Between National Culture, Societal Effectiveness and Desirable Leadership Attributes: A Brief Overview of the GLOBE Project 2004". Accessed November 2016. http://globe.bus.sfu.ca/study_2004_2007#data

Gouldner, A. W. 1960. "The Norm of Reciprocity: A Preliminary Statement." *American Sociological Review* 25 (2):161–78. doi: 10.2307/2092623.

Griffeth, R. W., P. W. Hom, and S. Gaertner. 2000. "A Meta-Analysis of Antecedents and Correlates of Employee Turnover: Update, Moderator Tests, and Research Implications for the Next Millennium." *Journal of Management* 26 (3):463–88. doi: 10.1177/014920630002600305.

Grover, S. L., and K. J. Crooker. 1995. "Who Appreciates Family-Responsive Human Resource Policies: The Impact of Family-Friendly Policies on the Organizational Attachment of Parents and Non-Parents." *Personnel Psychology* 48 (2):271–88. doi: 10.1111/j.1744-6570.1995.tb01757.x.

Harris, K. J., K. M. Kacmar, and L. A. Witt. 2005. "An Examination of the Curvilinear Relationship between Leader–Member Exchange and Intent to Turnover." *Journal of Organizational Behavior* 26 (4):363–78. doi: 10.1002/job.314.

Hauff, S., and N. Richter. 2015. " "Power Distance and Its Moderating Role in the Relationship between Situational Job Characteristics and Job Satisfaction: An Empirical Analysis Using Different Cultural Measures." *Cross Cultural Management: An International Journal* 22 (1):68–89. doi: 10.1108/CCM-11-2013-0164.

Hayes, A. F. 2006. "A Primer on Multilevel Modeling." *Human Communication Research* 32 (4):385–410. doi: 10.1111/j.1468-2958.2006.00281.x.

Hayton, J. C., G. Carnabuci, and R. Eisenberger. 2012. "With a Little Help from my Colleagues: A Social Embeddedness Approach to Perceived Organizational Support." *Journal of Organizational Behavior* 33 (2): 235–49. doi: 10.1002/job.755.

Hofstede, G. 1980. *Culture's Consequences: International Differences in Work-Related Values: Cross Cultural Research and Methodology Series.* (5th ed.). California: Sage publications.

Hofstede, G. 2001. *Culture's Consequences: Comparing Values, Behaviors, Institutions, and Organizations Across Nations.* (2nd ed.). California: Sage publications.

Holtom, B. C., T. R. Mitchell, T. W. Lee, and M. B. Eberly. 2008. "Turnover and Retention Research: A Glance at the past, a Closer Review of the Present, and a Venture into the Future." *The Academy of Management Annals* 2 (1):231–74. doi: 10.1080/19416520802211552.

House, R. J., P. J. Hanges, M. Javidan, P. W. Dorfman, and V. Gupta. 2004. *Culture, Leadership, and Organizations: The GLOBE Study of 62 Societies.* California: Sage Publications.

Hulin, C. L., M. Roznowski, and D. Hachiya. 1985. "Alternative Opportunities and Withdrawal Decisions: Empirical and Theoretical Discrepancies and an Integration." *Psychological Bulletin* 97 (2):233–50. doi: 10.1037/0033-2909.97.2.233.

International Labour Organization. 2016. "ILOSTAT Database – Definitions: Unemployment." Accessed November 2016. http://www.ilo.org/ilostat

Jung, Y., and N. Takeuchi. 2014. "Relationships among Leader–Member Exchange, Person–Organization Fit and Work Attitudes in Japanese and Korean Organizations: Testing a Cross-Cultural Moderating Effect." *The International Journal of Human Resource Management* 25 (1):23–46. doi: 10.1080/09585192.2013.778163.

Kahn, W. A. 1990. "Psychological Conditions of Personal Engagement and Disengagement at Work." *Academy of Management Journal* 33 (4):692–724. doi: 10.2307/256287.

Kalemci Tuzun, I., and R. Arzu Kalemci. 2012. "Organizational and Supervisory Support in Relation to Employee Turnover Intentions." *Journal of Managerial Psychology* 27 (5):518–34. doi: 10.1108/02683941211235418.

Kim, T. G., J. K. Lee, and J. H. Lee. 2013. "Do Interpersonal Relationships Still Matter for Turnover Intention? A Comparison of South Korea and China." *The International Journal of Human Resource Management* 24 (5): 966–84. doi: 10.1080/09585192.2012.743472.

Kirkman, B. L., G. Chen, J.-L. Farh, Z. X. Chen, and K. B. Lowe. 2009. "Individual Power Distance Orientation and Follower Reactions to Transformational Leaders: A Cross-Level, Cross-Cultural Examination." *Academy of Management Journal* 52 (4):744–64. doi: 10.5465/AMJ.2009.

Law, K. S., H. Wang, and C. Hui. 2010. "Currencies of Exchange and Global LMX: How They Affect Employee Task Performance and Extra-Role Performance." *Asia Pacific Journal of Management* 27 (4):625–46. doi: 10.1007/s10490-009-9141-8.

Liao, F., L. Yang, M. Wang, D. Drown, and J. Shi. 2013. "Team-Member Exchange and Work Engagement: Does Personality Make a Difference?" *Journal of Business and Psychology* 28 (1):63–77. doi: 10.1007/s10869-012-9266-5.

Liu, Y., R. Loi, and L. W. Lam. 2011. "Linking Organizational Identification and Employee Performance in Teams: The Moderating Role of Team-Member Exchange." *The International Journal of Human Resource Management* 22 (15):3187–201. doi: 10.1080/09585192.2011.560875.

May, D. R., R. L. Gilson, and L. M. Harter. 2004. "The Psychological Conditions of Meaningfulness, Safety and Availability and the Engagement of the Human Spirit at Work." *Journal of Occupational and Organizational Psychology* 77 (1):11–37. doi: 10.1348/096317904322915892.

Mitchell, T. R., B. C. Holtom, T. W. Lee, C. J. Sablynski, and M. Erez. 2001. "Why People Stay: Using Job Embeddedness to Predict Voluntary Turnover." *Academy of Management Journal* 44 (6):1102–21. doi: 10.2307/3069391.

Morris, M. W., and Z. Liu. 2015. "Psychological Functions of Subjective Norms Reference Groups, Moralization, Adherence, and Defiance." *Journal of Cross-Cultural Psychology* 46 (10):1279–87. doi: 10.1177/0022022115612161.

Mossholder, K. W., R. P. Settoon, and S. C. Henagan. 2005. "A Relational Perspective on Turnover: Examining Structural, Attitudinal, and Behavioral Predictors." *Academy of Management Journal* 48 (4):607–18. doi: 10.5465/amj.2005.17843941.

Muthen, L. K. 1999. "Intraclass Correlations." Accessed September 2017. http://www.statmodel.com/discussion/messages/12/18.html

Muthen, B., and A. Satorra. 1995. "Complex Sample Data in Structural Equation Modeling." *Sociological Methodology* 25:267–316. doi: 10.2307/271070.

Ng, T. W. H., and K. L. Sorensen. 2008. "Toward a Further Understanding of the Relationships between Perceptions of Support and Work Attitudes: A Meta-Analysis." *Group and Organization Management* 33 (3): 243–68. doi: 10.1177/1059601107313307.

Nishii, L. H., and D. M. Mayer. 2009. "Do Inclusive Leaders Help to Reduce Turnover in Diverse Groups? The Moderating Role of Leader–Member Exchange in the Diversity to Turnover Relationship." *Journal of Applied Psychology* 94 (6):1412–26. doi: 10.1037/a0017190.

OECD. 2005. "Glossary of Statistical Terms: Small and Medium-Sized Enterprises (SEMS)." Accessed September 2017. http://stats.oecd.org/glossary/

Perlow, L., and J. Weeks. 2002. "Who's Helping Whom? Layers of Culture and Workplace Behavior." *Journal of Organizational Behavior* 23 (4):345–61. doi: 10.1002/job.150.

Ramesh, A., and M. J. Gelfand. 2010. "Will They Stay or Will They Go? The Role of Job Embeddedness in Predicting Turnover in Individualistic and Collectivistic Cultures." *Journal of Applied Psychology* 95 (5):807–23. doi: 10.1037/a0019464.

Regts, G., and E. Molleman. 2013. "To Leave or Not to Leave: When Receiving Interpersonal Citizenship Behavior Influences an Employee's Turnover Intention." *Human Relations* 66 (2):193–218. doi: 10.1177/0018726712454311.

Rockstuhl, T., J. H. Dulebohn., S. Ang, and L. M. Shore. 2012. "Leader–Member Exchange (LMX) and Culture: A Meta-Analysis of Correlates of LMX across 23 Countries." *Journal of Applied Psychology* 97 (6):1097–130. doi: 10.1037/a0029978.

Saks, A. M. 2006. "Antecedents and Consequences of Employee Engagement." *Journal of Managerial Psychology* 21 (7):600–19. doi: 10.1108/02683940610690169.

Salancik, G. R., and J. Pfeffer. 1978. "A Social Information Processing Approach to Job Attitudes and Task Design." *Administrative Science Quarterly* 23 (2):224–53. doi: 10.2307/2392563.

Schaufeli, W. B., and A. B. Bakker. 2004. "Job Demands, Job Resources, and Their Relationship with Burnout and Engagement: A Multi-Sample Study." *Journal of Organizational Behavior* 25 (3):293–315. doi: 10.1002/job.248.

Seers, A. 1989. "Team-Member Exchange Quality: A New Construct for Role-Making Research." *Organizational Behavior and Human Decision Processes* 43 (1):118–35. doi: 10.1016/0749-5978(89)90060-5.

Shore, L. M., Coyle-Shapiro, J. A., X. Chen, and L. E. Tetrick. 2009. "Social Exchange in Work Settings: Content, Process, and Mixed Models." *Management and Organization Review* 5 (03):289–302. doi: 10.1111/j.1740-8784.2009.00158.x.

Steiner, D. D. 1988. "Value Perceptions in Leader-Member Exchange." *The Journal of Social Psychology* 128 (5): 611–8. doi: 10.1080/00224545.1988.9922915.

Sturman, M. C., L. Shao and J. H. Katz. 2012. "The Effect of Culture on the Curvilinear Relationship between Performance and Turnover." *Journal of Applied Psychology* 97 (1):46–62. doi: 10.1037/a0024868.

Taras, V., J. Rowney, and P. Steel. 2009. "Half a Century of Measuring Culture: Review of Approaches, Challenges, and Limitations Based on the Analysis of 121 Instruments for Quantifying Culture." *Journal of International Management* 15 (4):357–73. doi: 10.1016/j.intman.2008.08.005.

Triandis, H. C. 2001. "Individualism and Collectivism: Past, Present, and Future". In *The Handbook of Culture and Psychology*, edited by D. Matsumoto, 35–50. Oxford: University Press.

Tse, H., and M. T. Dasborough. 2008. "A Study of Exchange and Emotions in Team Member Relationships." *Group and Organization Management* 33 (2):194–215. doi: 10.1177/1059601106293779.

Tsui, A. S., S. S. Nifadkar, and A. Y. Ou. 2007. "Cross-National, Cross-Cultural Organizational Behavior Research: Advances, Gaps, and Recommendations." *Journal of Management* 33 (3):426–78. doi: 10.1177/0149206307300818.

van de Vijver, F., and K. Leung. 1997. "Methods and Data Analysis of Comparative Research". In *Handbook of Cross-Cultural Psychology*, 2nd ed., edited by J. W. Berry, Y. H. Poortinga, and J. Pandey, 257–300. Boston: Allyn & Bacon.

The Role of Perceived Development Opportunities on Affective Organizational Commitment of Older and Younger Nurses

Hanna Salminen and Merja Miettinen

Abstract: The research concerning human resource management (HRM) and organizational commitment is extensive. However, few studies have examined whether the relationship between employee perceptions of an organization's HR practices and work-related attitudes such as organizational commitment is moderated by age or career stage. This study examines the influence of perceived development opportunities and supervisory support on affective organizational commitment and whether this relationship is moderated by age or career stage. We collected the survey data from nurses in a Finnish university hospital ($N = 937$). The response rate was 54.4%. Our results show that the oldest nurses and those who had the longest organizational tenure were most affectively committed to the organization and had the highest rate of intention to remain at their current workplace. Affective organizational commitment was predicted by organizational tenure, skills that are appropriate for present work demands, supervisory support for development, and opportunities to use one's competencies. We detected no significant age-related interaction effects.

Public healthcare organizations in many countries are struggling with the increasing needs of an ageing population compounded with financial challenges (Buchan, O'May, and Dussault 2013). In addition, nursing staff are ageing, and many younger nurses are considering abandoning the profession (Flinkman et al. 2008; Buchan et al. 2013), In Finland, like in other Nordic countries, the total number of nurses is high. In 2015, Finland had more nurses (14.7) per capita (number of practicing nurses per 1,000 people) than the OECD average (9.0), even though the number of doctors and health expenditure per capita were close to the OECD average (OECD 2017). However, at that time, many Finnish nurses were due to retire shortly (Flinkman et al. 2008; Attree et al. 2011), and approximately 30% of Finnish nurses frequently consider changing their occupation (Flinkman et al. 2008).

Recent studies have stressed that retaining nurses is one of the best ways to solve the current nursing shortage (Armstrong-Stassen and Schlosser 2010; Attree et al. 2011). In practice, this means using the skills and competencies of the available nursing resources more effectively (Buchan et al. 2013). However, this requires age-sensitive HR practices to promote the retention of differently aged employees (Armstrong-Stassen and Schlosser 2010). In general, HRM scholars have paid more attention to age-related issues in recent years (Kooij et al. 2014). Some researchers have taken an employer-level perspective and analyzed current HR practices and the need for age-sensitive practices. Other studies have focused on employees' evaluations of HR practices in their organizations (Kooij et al. 2014). For example, recent studies have demonstrated that perceived development opportunities are positively related to employees' work-related attitudes such as affective organizational commitment, which in turn is positively related to nurses' intentions to remain in the organization (Armstrong-Stassen and Schlosser 2008) and negatively associated with their intention to leave the profession (Laine 2005; Flinkman et al. 2008).

As a result of these studies, a number of HR practices important for retaining older and younger employees have been identified. However, these studies have also been criticized for lacking a solid theoretical background in terms of HRM (Armstrong-Stassen and Schlosser 2010; Kooij et al. 2014). For example, the authors rarely explain the mechanisms by which HR practices influence the retention of different aged employees in detail (Armstrong-Stassen and Schlosser 2010). Some scholars have argued that HR practices may not directly influence employees' intentions to stay in or leave the organization; rather, these intentions are mediated by work-related attitudes, such as affective organizational commitment (Armstrong-Stassen and Schlosser 2010). There is also scant research concerning whether the relationship between perceived HR practices and organizational commitment is moderated by age (Kooij et al. 2010) or career stage (Finegold et al. 2002; Conway 2004).

This study builds on HRM literature and views HR practices from an employee-level perspective. More specifically, we focus on the significance of perceived development opportunities and supervisory support for nurses' affective organizational commitment. We analyze whether this relationship is moderated by age or career stage. Opportunities for development and supervisory support have been identified as important factors for the retention of older (Lavoie-Tremblay et al. 2006) and younger nurses (Flinkman et al. 2008). We are interested in finding out whether perceived developmental opportunities and supervisory support significantly enhance the affective organizational commitment of nurses of all ages.

THEORETICAL BACKGROUND

Organizational commitment is a central work-related attitude, and its importance has been widely acknowledged in the field of HRM. Allen and Meyer (1996, 252) have defined organizational commitment as "*a psychological link between the employee and his or her organization that makes it less likely that the employee will voluntarily leave the organization.*" Some researchers have seen organizational commitment as a unidimensional concept such as Mowday et al. (1979). However, Meyer and Allen (1991) have defined organizational commitment as a multidimensional construct consisting of *affective*, *normative*, and *continuance* components. Affective commitment refers to emotional fondness towards the organization, normative commitment relates to the feeling of obligation, and continuance commitment denotes awareness of the costs related to leaving the current workplace (Meyer and Allen 1991; Conway 2004).

A meta-analysis by Mathieu and Zajac (1990) has demonstrated that organizational commitment increases with age and organizational tenure. Conway (2004) has argued that those who work longer in an organization internalize the organizations values' more thoroughly. On the other hand, family responsibilities may influence how easily older employees are able to leave the organization (Finegold et al. 2002). There is also evidence that better educated employees tend to be less committed to the organization (Mathieu and Zajac 1990; Swailes 2002).

As a concept, organizational commitment and especially affective commitment is closely related to work engagement. They are both seen to influence employees' job performance and retention (Chalofsky and Krishna 2009, 190). While organizational commitment relates to employees' attitudinal responses towards workplace, work engagement captures employees' energetic, dedicated, and enthusiastic ways to focus on work (Hallberg and Schaufeli 2006). In other words, work engagement describes employees' "optimal functioning" and it has been studied more in the context of health issues, whereas organizational commitment has been examined in the context of retention (Hallberg and Schaufeli 2006, 120–121). Chalofsky and Krishna (2009) have argued that, in the current working life, committed and engaged employees are needed for effective performance of organizations.

High-commitment HRM literature stresses that HR practices can be used to retain employees in the organization (Conway 2004). This literature relies on both the configurational and best practice perspective. The former emphasizes the identification and implementation of "bundles" of HR practices to improve organizational performance and employees' work-related attitudes. The latter stresses that certain universal HR practices are beneficial for all kinds of organizations in general. Usually, these so-called high-commitment HR practices are divided into three categories: opportunities to participate, performance-based incentives, and the development of skills and competencies (Conway 2004, 417–418).

In this study, we focus on employees' opportunities to develop their skills and competencies, which have been identified as an important part of HRM in terms of retaining older employees (Walker 2005). We understand competencies as the balance between job demands and an employee's ability do his or her job (Lehto and Järnefelt 2000). Recently, researchers have examined opportunities to develop one's competencies broadly, covering both opportunities for formal training as well as opportunities for informal learning (Van der Heijden, Gorgievski, and De Lange 2016) and opportunities for career development are seen to include both vertical and lateral job movements (Armstrong-Stassen 2008). Studies of the retention of older employees have also stressed that for professional competence development, older employees need encouragement and support from their supervisor (Ilmarinen 2006; Armstrong-Stassen and Schlosser 2010). Supervisory support may include, for example, giving feedback, providing career guidance, providing challenging work tasks, and opportunities for development (van der Heijden 2003; van der Heijden et al. 2010). For example, Armstrong-Stassen and Schlosser (2010) have demonstrated that affective organizational commitment mediated the relationship between older nurses' perceived organizational support and their intentions to continue working in their current workplace.

Some HRM scholars have stressed that the significance of an organization's training and development practices should not only be seen as improving employees' competencies, but also as influencing their work-related attitudes (Bartlett 2001). The notion that high commitment HR practices are related to work-related attitudes such as organizational commitment, through employees' perceptions of them, is rooted in social exchange theory (Bartlett 2001; Kooij et al. 2010, 2014). According to this theory, HR practices demonstrate to employees that the organization values their work, and employees respond to this by showing stronger commitment to the organization (Armstrong-Stassen 2008; Armstrong-Stassen and Schlosser 2010). In other words, employees may perceive the development opportunities provided by the organization as rewards (De Gieter et al. 2012). However, social exchange theory suggests that the value of HR practices may differ among employees, according to age or career stage, for example (Kooij et al. 2010; Finegold et al. 2002).

Traditional career stage models suggest that employees pass through different phases during their working career, which can influence their work-related needs and expectations (Finegold et al. 2002). For example, Super (1957) has identified four career stages and defined them as *exploration, establishment, maintenance,* and *disengagement.* Exploration means finding one's own place at work (Finegold et al. 2002). For example, there is evidence that nurses who are in the exploration stage more often consider leaving their profession (Flinkman et al. 2008, 2010). Establishment includes stabilization and growth, in the form of extending one's professional role in the organization, for example (Finegold et al. 2002). During the maintenance stage, employees often focus on retaining interest in their current job, and they use their own resources more efficiently in terms of work experience. During the disengagement stage, mentoring roles, providing guidance to younger colleagues, and gradual withdrawal from working life are important factors (Finegold et al. 2002; Conway 2004).

Few HRM studies have paid attention to the question of whether the relationship between perceived HR practices and work-related attitudes is moderated by age (Finegold et al. 2002; Kooij et al. 2010) or career stage (Conway 2004). Kooij et al. (2010, 1128), in their meta-analysis of 83 studies, demonstrated that employee perceptions of HR practices were positively related to work-related attitudes, and that this relationship was moderated by chronological age. In their study, they distinguished between maintenance and development HR practices. Maintenance HR practices involve, for example, job security, rewards, and benefits, information sharing, working in teams, and flexible work schemes. Development HR practices relate to training and development, internal promotion, career progress, and job enrichment. Relying on the lifespan theory of selection, optimization, and compensation (SOC), which assumes that as they age, people try simultaneously to maximize the gains and minimize the losses brought by ageing, Kooij and her colleagues expected that the associations between development HR practices and affective organizational commitment would weaken as employees grew older. This hypothesis was supported for the association between promotion and affective organizational commitment (Kooij et al. 2010). Conway's (2004) study in the Irish financial sector demonstrated that the relationship between perceived career development opportunities and normative organizational commitment was strongest among those employees who were in the early stage of their career. Similarly, Finegold et al. (2002) demonstrated that satisfaction with opportunities to develop competencies had a stronger negative relationship with turnover intentions in technical workers under 30 than those over 45. However, the interaction effects were rather small (Finegold et al. 2002).

Many recent HRM studies have questioned the significance of so-called "universal" HR practices at individual level, and have argued that the significance of different HR practices for the retention of employees may vary according to individual differences, such as age or career stage (Conway 2004; Kooij et al. 2014). Previous studies (Finegold et al. 2002; Conway 2004; Kooij et al. 2010) suggest that younger employees may value the development opportunities provided by their organization more than older employees. This is because younger employees are at a stage where they need to develop their organization-specific competencies (Finegold et al. 2002). However, career development opportunities can be greater during the mid-career stage, when the focus is on career establishment (Conway 2004; Finegold et al. 2002). On the other hand, Hall and Mirvis (1996) have argued that traditional organizational careers are becoming rarer and are being replaced by so-called "protean careers," which include continuous learning during the whole career (Finegold et al. 2002). This indicates that development opportunities and especially opportunities to develop and use one's professional competencies will be crucial for both older and younger employees.

In this study, we distinguish between older and younger employees chronologically. We adopt the age of 45 as a starting point when referring to older employees, which is in accordance with earlier studies (Brough et al. 2011; Ilmarinen 2006). This criterion is based on the notion that this is often the time when employees' work ability and career aspirations begin to change significantly, although individual differences are great (Ilmarinen 2006; Buyens et al. 2009). In this study, we use organizational tenure to indicate career stage, divided into four categories: less than two years, between two and 10 years, 11–20 years, and over 20 years; this roughly resembles the career stages presented by Super (1957).

This study has two objectives. The first is to examine age-related differences in terms of intention to remain at the current workplace and affective organizational commitment. The second is to explore the relationship between perceived HR practices and affective organizational commitment, and to analyze whether this relationship is moderated by age or career stage.

RESEARCH PROCESS

Procedure and Participants

We gathered the research data between December 2006 and January 2007 from registered nurses and nursing personnel working in a public university hospital in Finland. The hospital's ethical committee gave their permission for the study. The nurses we studied were permanently or temporarily employed, and they worked in non-managerial positions in the surgical or psychiatric care wards at the hospital. We distributed 937 questionnaires via the hospital's internal post. Respondents received a personally addressed envelope containing a 12-page questionnaire and a return envelope. They also received one follow-up letter.

TABLE 1.
The Background Characteristics of the Respondents % (*n*).

Age, mean ± SD	*41.5 ± 9.7*
Age groups, % (*n*)	
Under 35	29 (146)
35–44	30 (153)
45–54	30 (155)
Over 54	11 (56)
Organizational tenure, % (*n*)	
under 2 years	8 (40)
2–10 years	37 (190)
10–20 years	36 (180)
over 20 years	19 (93)
Gender, % (n)	
Women	83 (423)
Men	17 (87)
Education, % (*n*)	
College level or lower	69 (346)
Bachelors' degree or upper	31 (158)
Profession, % (*n*)	
Registered nurses	82 (415)
Other nursing personnel	18 (95)
Form of employment, % (*n*)	
Permanent	75 (384)
Temporary	25 (120)
Working time, % (*n*)	
Shift work	74 (375)
Day work	26 (133)
Pay €/month, mean ± SD	2145 ± 332
Division of care, % (*n*)	
Operative	71 (363)
Psychiatric	29 (147)

In total, 510 questionnaires were returned. The response rate was 54.4%. No statistically significant differences were found between respondents and non-respondents in terms of demographic data, indicating that no systematic bias occurred among respondents. We present the background characteristics of the respondents in Table 1.

The mean age of the respondents was 41.5 years, within a range of 21–62 years. The majority of the respondents were female (83%) and over half of them (54%) had worked for over 10 years in the current organization. Most of the informants were registered nurses, and the rest were other nursing personnel. Of the respondents, 71% worked in the surgical wards and 29% worked in the psychiatric care wards. Most of the respondents (75%) were permanently employed.

Measures

Age was operationalized as calendar age. Organizational tenure was used to indicate career stage. Respondents were asked to state their tenure (years and months) in their current organization. We subsequently divided this variable into four categories: (1) less than 2 years, (2) between 2 and 10 years, (3) 11–20 years, (4) >20 years, based on the career stages presented by Super (1957).

Ability to do one's job was measured by asking respondents to indicate what they felt was their skills level. The response scale was: (1) "I need additional training in order to perform well in my current job"; (2) "my skills are appropriate for my current work demands"; (3) "I have the potential to carry out more challenging tasks" (Lehto and Järnefelt 2000).

We based our affective organizational commitment scale on Allen and Meyer (1990) scale. It comprised a 5-point Likert scale, from (1) totally disagree to (5) totally agree, with higher scores indicating higher levels of organizational commitment. Affective organizational commitment was measured using eight items. These included, for example, "I would be very happy spending the rest of my career with this organization."

Intention to remain was examined using one item: "I will continue working here for as long as possible," which is almost identical to the item used by Armstrong-Stassen and Schlosser (2008). We used a 5-point Likert scale, with higher scores indicating higher intent to remain (1 = totally disagree, 2 = somewhat disagree, 3 = neither agree nor disagree, 4 = somewhat agree, and 5 = totally agree). We then converted this scale into a three-point scale: disagree, neither agree nor disagree, and agree.

The scale used to assess perceived development opportunities consisted of 13 items, which we collected from earlier studies concerning perceived development opportunities for nurses (Armstrong-Stassen and Cameron 2005) and employees in different occupations (Lehto and Järnefelt 2000; Tikkanen et al. 2002; Tuomi and Vanhala 2002). We used a 5-point response scale for the items, varying from (1) very poor to (5) very good. We conducted principal component analysis with Varimax-rotation to find the possible dimensions of perceived development opportunities (KMO value = 0. 834, Bartlett's test $p < 0.001$). Two items did not load well, and they were dropped. Eleven items loaded on three factors: (1) opportunities for professional competence development, (2) opportunities to use one's competencies, and (3) opportunities for career progress (Table 2).

TABLE 2.
Factor Loading Structure for Perceived Development Opportunities

Rotated component matrix	1	2	3
Opportunity to receive training that promotes professional competencies	0.828		
Opportunity to participate during working time in training provided by the employer	0.796		
Opportunity to develop one's professional competencies	0.869		
Opportunity to learn new things	0.738		
Opportunity to get guidance related to the work	0.676		
Opportunity to use knowledge and skills gained through professional training		0.663	
Opportunity to use knowledge and skills gained through work experience		0.819	
Opportunity to choose own working methods and develop these		0.746	
Opportunity for career progress			0.782
Opportunity to move from work assignment to another work task that is at the same level			0.707
Opportunity to progress to more challenging work tasks			0.872

Rotated component matrix	
My supervisor tells me about the available opportunities for professional competence development	0.754
Supervisor encourages me to participate in training and development activities in the workplace	0.863
Supervisor supports me in learning new things	0.857
Supervisor discusses my development goals with me regularly	0.726
Supervisor rewards me based on my development	0.690
Supervisor plans my work so that I have an opportunity to develop within it	0.751
Supervisor treats me with fairly in terms of training and development matters	0.819
Supervisor provides equal development opportunities for all employees	0.793

The items were developed from earlier studies because we did not find previously validated measures for perceived development opportunities. These eleven items explained 68.3% of the variance. The mean values for perceived opportunities to develop and use one's competencies were rather high. However, the mean values for perceived opportunities for career progress were low.

We developed the scale for perceived supervisory support for development using the items noted by Armstrong-Stassen and Cameron (2005), London (1993), Maurer and Tarulli (1994), Maurer et al. (2003), and van der Heijden (2003). We used a 5-point Likert scale for these eight items, varying from (1) totally disagree to (5) totally agree. We conducted a principal component factor analysis with Varimax-rotation (KMO value = 0.889, Bartlett's test $p < 0.001$). All items loaded on one factor, which we termed perceived supervisory support for development (Table 3).

Data Analysis

We conducted statistical analyses using SPSS Statistics 20.0. We performed the χ^2-test and one-way analysis of variance (ANOVA) to study possible age and career stage differences in the intentions to remain at the same place of work and in terms of affective organizational commitment. The test of variance homogeneity (Levene's test) showed that the variances were equal. We measured the bivariate correlations between studied variables using Spearman correlation. We performed hierarchical regression analysis (Stepwise) to determine the proportion of variance in the dependent variable (affective organizational commitment) predicted by the independent variables. In the regression analysis, we investigated interaction effects similarly to previous studies (Finegold et al. 2002; Conway 2004) and we controlled for educational level and gender. In addition, we assessed multicollinearity; it was not a problem in this study.

RESULTS

In total, 43% of the nurses surveyed agreed totally or partly with the statement "I will continue working here for as long as possible" (Table 4). However, almost half of the

TABLE 4.
Age-Related Differences in Terms of Intention to Remain in the Workplace

	Disagree	Neither agree nor disagree	Agree
	% (n)	% (n)	% (n)
Age group			
Under 35	47% (68)	20% (28)	33% (47)
35–44	35% (53)	25% (37)	40% (60)
45–54	25% (38)	26% (40)	49% (76)
Over 54	31% (17)	13% (7)	56% (31)
Totally	35% (176)	22% (112)	43% (209)
Organizational tenure			
Under 2 years	38% (15)	18% (7)	44% (17)
2–10 years	42% (78)	27% (50)	31% (58)
11–20 years	32% (57)	20% (36)	48% (86)
Over 20 years	28% (25)	20% (18)	52% (48)
Total	35% (175)	22% (111)	43% (209)

TABLE 5.
Age-Related Differences in Terms of Affective Organizational Commitment

	Mean	SD	F-test	df	sig
Age group					
Under 35	2.824	0.722			
35–44	2.945	0.799			
45–54	3.042	0.788			
Over 54	3.396	0.697	7.773	3	0.001
Organizational tenure					
Under 2 years	2.760	0.756			
2–10 years	2.825	0.723			
10–20 years	3.019	0.824			
over 20 years	3.314	0.688	9.508	3	0.001

respondents under 35 (47%) disagreed with the statement totally or partly. There was a statistical difference between age groups and intention to remain at the current workplace ($\chi^2 = 22.923$ $df = 6$, $p = 0.001$). Respondents in the oldest age group (over 54) had the strongest intentions to remain at their current workplace.

The relationship between organizational tenure categories and intention to remain in the current workplace was also statistically significant ($\chi^2 = 16.526$, $df = 6$, $p = 0.011$), indicating that those who had the longest tenure were most intent on remaining in their current workplace. However, nurses in the establishment stage of their career (who had worked in the organization for between two and 10 years) were least intent on remaining in their current workplace.

There were statistically significant differences between age groups in the level of affective organizational commitment ($F = 7.773$, $df = 3$, $p = 0.001$) and organizational tenure ($F = 9.508$, $df = 3$, $p = 0.001$). The oldest nurses, and those with the longest organizational tenure, were most committed to the organization affectively (Table 5).

TABLE 6.
Means, Standard Deviations, Reliability Estimates and Bivariate Correlations

Variables	Mean	SD	α	1	2	3	4	5	6	7	8	9
1) Intention to remain	3.06	1.260										
2) Affective organizational commitment	2.988	0.779	0.829	0.512** (n=494)								
3) Age	41.52	9.739		0.190** (n=502)	0.193** (n=496)							
4) Organizational tenure	12.74	9.011		0.143** (n=495)	0.209** (n=489)	0.719** (n=503)						
5) Opportunities to develop one's professional competencies	3.718	0.647	0.871	0.168** (n=495)	0.299** (n=490)	-0.022 (n=500)	-0.070 (n=493)					
6) Opportunities for use one's professional competencies	3.878	0.623	0.742	0.146** (n=497)	0.275** (n=492)	-0.058 (n=502)	-0.022 (n=495)	0.441** (n=497)				
7) Opportunities for career progress	2.706	0.819	0.775	0.153** (n=496)	0.227** (n=491)	-0.194** (n=501)	-0.143** (n=494)	0.387** (n=496)	0.326** (n=499)			
8) Supervisory support for development	3.146	0.855	0.908	0.204** (n=489)	0.394** (n=487)	0.074 (n=494)	0.036 (n=487)	0.551** (n=488)	0.405** (n=490)	0.415** (n=489)		
9) Competence at doing one's job	2.08	0.713		-0.118** (n=501)	-0.079 (n=495)	0.011 (n=508)	0.114* (n=501)	-0.030 (n=499)	-0.011 (n=501)	-0.079 (n=500)	-0.142** (n=493)	

Statistically significant correlation coefficients ($p < 0.05$) are marked in bold.
*$p < 0.05$; **$p < 0.01$.

TABLE 7.
Hierarchical Regression (Stepwise) of Affective Organizational Commitment

Variables	Affective organizational commitment (Standardized beta coefficient)
Organizational tenure	0.211***
Skills in balance with present work demands	0.102*
Perceived supervisory support for development	0.325***
Perceived opportunities to use one's competencies	0.149**
N	456
R^2	0.241
Adjusted R^2	0.234
F-test	36.159***
df	4
Standard error of estimate	0.682
Durbin–Watson	1.928

$^*p < 0.05$; $^{**}p < 0.01$; $^{***}p < 0.001$.

Table 6 provides descriptive statistics and Spearman correlations. All Cronbach's α-values were over 0.70, which can be considered satisfactory. Affective organizational commitment related positively and strongly with intention to remain in the current workplace ($r = 0.512$, $p < 0.01$). The level of affective organizational commitment was moderate (mean = 2.988). In terms of personal variables, age and organizational tenure correlated positively with affective organizational commitment, indicating that older nurses and those who had worked longer in the organization were more affectively committed to the organization than younger ones. Perceived development opportunities and supervisory support for development were positively and significantly related to affective organizational commitment.

We performed a hierarchical multiple regression analysis with the Stepwise method to examine the antecedents of affective organizational commitment. We entered personal variables (age, organizational tenure, education, gender, ability to do one's job) in the first block. We then entered opportunities to develop and use one's professional competencies, opportunities for career progress, and supervisory support for development. We entered the interaction terms in the final block; we created these by multiplying perceived HR practices by age and by organizational tenure categories. In total, we used 16 interaction terms in the analysis. We present Standardized coefficients (β), the proportion of the variance explained (R^2), and adjusted R^2 for the model, in Table 7.

Table 7 shows that four variables predicted almost 25% of the variance in affective organizational commitment. Our results show that longer organizational tenure, appropriate skills for present work demands, positive perceptions of supervisory support for development, and opportunities to use one's competencies were positively related to affective organizational commitment. Perceived supervisory support for development predicted affective organizational commitment most strongly. None of the interactions in terms of age or career stage reached significance in the regression model.

CONCLUSIONS

Recent studies have consistently stressed that for public health care organizations, one of the best ways to respond to the shortage of nurses is to retain and make greater use of their existing nurses (Armstrong-Stassen and Schlosser 2010; Estryn-Behar et al. 2010; Buchan et al. 2013). This requires age-sensitive HR practices to retain both older and younger nurses (Lavoie-Tremblay et al. 2006). Based on the notion that perceived HR practices may not have a direct effect on employees' intentions to stay in or leave the organization, we focused in this study on the significance of perceived development opportunities and supervisory support for the affective organizational commitment of nurses. For example, Armstrong-Stassen and Schlosser (2010) have argued that HR practices can influence employees' withdrawal intentions indirectly rather than directly. In addition, we examined whether the relationship between perceived HR practices and affective organizational commitment differs according to age or career stage.

In line with previous studies, our results demonstrated that the oldest nurses and those who had worked longest for their current employer were most affectively committed to the organization (Mathieu and Zajac 1990; Laine 2005). Affective organizational commitment was positively associated with intentions to remain at the present organization, indicating that more affectively committed nurses are less likely to leave their employer. Based on social exchange theory, we expected positive associations between perceived HR practices and affective organizational commitment. Our results partly support this assumption. In the regression analysis, affective organizational commitment was predicted by organizational tenure, appropriate skills for current job demands, supervisory support for development, and opportunities to use one's competencies.

These results support previous age management studies that stress the importance of a balance between individual-level competencies and job demands (Walker 2005; Ilmarinen 2006). For example, Estryn-Behar et al. (2010) found that nurses' dissatisfaction with the use of their competencies and lack of autonomy were significant reasons for leaving their profession, whereas the study of Laine et al. (2011) showed that the work content and workplace atmosphere were the most significant factors related to Finnish nurses' organizational commitment. The results of our study also lend support to previous studies that emphasize the importance of social support, especially quality of leadership, in the retention of nurses (Van der Heijden, van Dam, and Hasselhorn 2009; Armstrong-Stassen and Schlosser 2010). For example, Bartlett's (2001) study demonstrated that perceived supervisory support for training had a positive association with nurses' affective organizational commitment.

In our study, perceived opportunities to develop one's competencies and opportunities for career progress had a non-significant effect on affective organizational commitment in the regression model. The significance of competence development opportunities for nurses' affective organizational commitment might be reduced because nurses may perceive training and development opportunities provided by the organization as standard job conditions (De Gieter et al. 2012). In general, Finnish nurses have rather limited promotion opportunities (Laine et al. 2011). For that reason, opportunities for career progress may not be important for their affective organizational commitment. In addition, due to the emotionally and physically demanding nature of the nursing profession (van der Heijden et al. 2009), we might assume that interpersonal relations at work, such as supervisory support, are more important for nurses' affective organizational commitment than formal training opportunities, for example.

Contrary to earlier studies (Finegold et al. 2002; Conway 2004; Kooij et al. 2010), we detected no statistically significant age or career-stage interaction effects. This result indicates that there are more similarities than differences between older and younger nurses in terms of the importance of perceived development opportunities and supervisory support. As the study by Finegold et al. (2002) suggests, researchers might pay too much attention to differences between age groups or career stages. Our finding also supports the notion of protean career (Hall and Mirvis 1996), implying that possibilities to fully use one's professional competencies are crucial for both older and younger nurses.

Implications for Practice

This study provides empirical evidence of a strong positive relationship between affective organizational commitment and intention to remain in the current workplace. Therefore, it can be assumed that nurses' perceptions of HR practices can indirectly influence their intention to stay with their organization via affective organizational commitment. The results show that opportunities to fully use one's professional competencies can be used as a way of enhancing both older and younger nurses' affective commitment to the organization. These opportunities include using professional competencies gained through training or work experiences and the ability to influence and develop one's working methods. In addition, supervisors can enhance the affective organizational commitment of both older and younger nurses by supporting and encouraging their development. Together these practices may help to retain nursing staff. Primarily, opportunities to use one's competencies are important for two reasons. First, they are important for maintaining and developing employees' professional competencies and abilities. Second, they can be used to strengthen nurses' affective commitment towards their organization.

Limitations and Suggestions for Future Research

While our study offers some insights into the relationship between perceived HR practices and affective organizational commitment, it was restricted to a female dominated profession and to a Finnish university hospital. Therefore, caution is required with regard to generalizing the results. Second, the cross-sectional nature of the study made it impossible to verify the causality of the variables studied. Based on social exchange theory, we assumed that HR practices perceived as good could enhance nurses' affective commitment to the organization. However, the opposite causality is also possible. A longitudinal research design is needed to confirm the causes of the relationships.

The use of a single item for measuring intention to remain in the current workplace may have reduced the reliability of this instrument. It should be also noted that we studied nurses' perceptions of development opportunities and supervisory support, which may not reflect actual practice in the hospital. However, it is likely that subjective perceptions of HR practices are linked to individuals' work-related attitudes, such as organizational commitment (Armstrong-Stassen 2008). A further point is that the data were self-reported and from a single questionnaire, making this study vulnerable to common-method bias (Podsakoff et al. 2003).

Future studies could investigate the effect of other HR practices on the work-related attitudes of employees of different ages. A configurational approach to HRM assumes that bundles of HR practices may have stronger effects on employees' work-related attitudes than individual HR practices (Armstrong-Stassen and Schlosser 2010; Kooij et al. 2010, 2014). For example, perceptions of HR practices aiming to improve the work-life balance could be significant for the retention of nurses. Finally, the use of different outcome variables, such as work engagement could be an important avenue for future research.

ACKNOWLEDGEMENTS

This study is based on the PhD thesis of the first author, and she would like to thank the Ellen and Artturi Nyyssönen Foundation and the Foundation for Economic Education for the funding.

The authors also thank EIASM for organizing the Workshop for Strategic Human Resource Management that provided the opportunity to engage in this discussion. We also thank the French Investissements d'Avenir (ANR-11-IDEX-0003/Labex Ecodec/ANR-11-LABX-0047) for funding our working meetings to produce this article. Additionally, we thank HEC Paris School of Management and NEOMA Business School for their support of our research.

REFERENCES

Allen, N. J., and J. P. Meyer. 1990. "The Measurement and Antecedents of Affective, Continuance, and Normative Commitment to the Organization." *Journal of Occupational Psychology* 63 (1):1–18. doi:10.1111/j.2044-8325.1990.tb00506.x.

Allen, N. J., and J. P. Meyer. 1996. "Affective, Continuance, and Normative Commitment to the Organization: An Examination of Construct Validity." *Journal of Vocational Behavior* 49 (3):252–76. doi:10.1006/jvbe.1996.0043.

Armstrong-Stassen, M. 2008. "Factors Associated with Job Content Plateauing among Older Workers." *Career Development International* 13 (7):594–613. doi:10.1108/13620430810911074.

Armstrong-Stassen, M., and S. J. Cameron. 2005. "Concerns, Satisfaction, and Retention of Canadian Community Health Nurses." *Journal of Community Health Nursing* 22 (4):181–94. doi:10.1207/s15327655jchn2204_1.

Armstrong-Stassen, M., and F. Schlosser. 2008. "Benefits of a Supportive Development Climate for Older Workers." *Journal of Managerial Psychology* 23 (4):419–37. doi:10.1108/02683940810869033.

Armstrong-Stassen, M., and F. Schlosser. 2010. "When Hospitals Provide HR Practices Tailored to Older Nurses, Will Older Nurses Stay? It May Depend on Their Supervisor." *Human Resource Management Journal* 20 (4): 375–90. doi:10.1111/j.1748-8583.2010.00143.x.

Attree, M., M. Flinkman, B. Howley, R.-L. Lakanmaa, M. Lima-Basto, and L. Uhrenfeldt. 2011. "A Review of Nursing Workforce Policies in Five European Countries: Denmark, Finland, Ireland, Portugal and United Kingdom." *Journal of Nursing Management* 19 (6):786–802. doi:10.1111/j.1365-2834.2011.01214.x.

Bartlett, K. R. 2001. "The Relationship between Training and Organizational Commitment: A Study in the Health Care Field." *Human Resource Development Quarterly* 12 (4):335–52. doi:10.1002/hrdq.1001.

Brough, P., G. Johnson, S. Drummond, S. Pennisi, and C. Timms. 2011. "Comparisons of Cognitive Ability and Job Attitudes of Older and Younger Workers." *Equality, Diversity and Inclusion: An International Journal* 30 (2): 105–26. doi:10.1108/02610151111116508.

Buchan, J., F. O'May, and G. Dussault. 2013. "Nursing Workforce Policy and the Economic Crisis: A Global Overview." *Journal of Nursing Scholarship* 45 (3):298–307. doi:10.1111/jnu.12028.

Buyens, D., H. V. Dijk, T. Dewilde, and A. De Vos. 2009. "The Aging Workforce: Perceptions of Career Ending." *Journal of Managerial Psychology* 24 (2):102–17. doi:10.1108/02683940910928838.

Chalofsky, N., and V. Krishna. 2009. "Meaningfulness, Commitment, and Engagement: The Intersection of a Deeper Level of Intrinsic Motivation." *Advances in Developing Human Resources* 11 (2):189–203. doi:10.1177/1523422309333147.

Conway, E. 2004. "Relating Career Stage to Attitudes Towards HR Practices and Commitment: Evidence of Interaction Effects?" *European Journal of Work and Organizational Psychology* 13 (4):417–46. doi:10.1080/13594320444000155.

De Gieter, S., R. De Cooman, J. Hofmans, R. Pepermans, and M. Jegers. 2012. "Pay-Level Satisfaction and Psychological Reward Satisfaction as Mediators of the Organizational Justice-Turnover Intention Relationship." *International Studies of Management and Organization* 42 (1):50–67. doi:10.2753/IMO0020-8825420103.

Estryn-Behar, M., B. I. J. M. van der Heijden, C. Fry, and H.-M. Hasselhorn. 2010. "Longitudinal Analysis of Personal and Work-Related Factors Associated with Turnover among Nurses." *Nursing Research* 59 (3):166–77. doi:10.1097/NNR.0b013e3181dbb29f.

Finegold, D., S. Mohrman, and G. Spreitzer. 2002. "Age Effects on the Predictors of Technical Workers' Commitment and Willingness to Turnover." *Journal of Organizational Behavior* 23 (5):655–74. doi:10.1002/job.159.

Flinkman, M., M. Laine, H. Leino-Kilpi, H.-M. Hasselhorn, and S. Salanterä. 2008. "Explaining Young Registered Finnish Nurses' Intention to Leave the Profession: A Questionnaire Survey." *International Journal of Nursing Studies* 45 (5):727–39. doi:10.1016/j.ijnurstu.2006.12.006.

Flinkman, M., M. Laine, H. Leino-Kilpi, and S. Salanterä. 2010. "Nurses' Intention to Leave the Profession: Integrative Review." *Journal of Advanced Nursing* 66 (7):1422–34. doi:10.1111/j.1365-2648.2010.05322.x.

Hall, D. T., and P. Mirvis. 1996. "The New Protean Career: Psychological Success and the Path with Heart. In. *The Career Is Dead, Long Live the Career*, edited by D. T. Hall, San Francisco, CA: Jossey-Bass.

Hallberg, U. E., and W. B. Schaufeli. 2006. "Same Same" But Different?" *European Psychologist* 11 (2):119–27. doi:10.1027/1016-9040.11.2.119.

Ilmarinen, J. 2006. *Towards a Longer Worklife—Ageing and the Quality of Worklife in the European Union*. Helsinki: Finnish Institute of Occupational Health.

Kooij, D. T. A. M., P. G. W. Jansen, J.S.E. Dikkers, and A. H. de Lange. 2014. "Managing Aging Works: A Mixed Methods Study on Bundles of HR Practices for Aging Workers." *The International Journal of Human Resource Management* 25 (15):2192–2212. doi:10.1080/09585192.2013.872169.

Kooij, D. T. A. M., P. G. W. Jansen, J. S. E. Dikkers, and A. H. de Lange. 2010. "The Influence of Age on the Associations between HR Practices and Both Affective Commitment and Job Satisfaction." *Journal of Organizational Behavior* 31 (8):1111–36. doi:10.1002/job.666.

Laine, M. 2005. *Hoitajana Huomennakin. Hoitajien Työpaikkaan ja Ammattiin Sitoutuminen (As a Nurse Also Tomorrow. Organisational and Professional Commitment of Nurses). Doctoral Dissertation. Annales Universitatis Turkuensis C 233*. Turku: University of Turku.

Laine, M., K. Kokkinen, A. Kaarlela-Tuomaala, E. Valtanen, M. Elovainio, M. Keinänen, and R. Suomi. 2011. *Sosiaali- ja Terveysalan Työolot 2010 (The Working Conditions and Well-being of Social and Health Care Staff 2010)*. Helsinki: Finnish Institute of Occupational Health.

Lavoie-Tremblay, M., L. O'Brien-Pallas, C. Viens, L. H. Brabant, and C. Gélinas. 2006. "Towards an Integrated Approach for Management of Ageing Nurses." *Journal of Nursing Management* 14 (3):207–12. doi:10.1111/j.1365-2934.2006.00604.x.

Lehto, A.-M. and N. Järnefelt. 2000. *Jaksaen ja Joustaen. Artikkeleita Työolotutkimuksesta. (Managing and Bending. Essays of the Working Conditions)*. Helsinki: Statistics Finland.

London, M. 1993. "Relationships between Career Motivation, Empowerment and Support for Career Development." *Journal of Occupational and Organizational Psychology* 66 (1):55–69. doi:10.1111/j.2044-8325.1993.tb00516.x.

Mathieu, J. E., and D. M. Zajac. 1990. "A Review and Meta-Analysis of the Antecedents, Correlates, and Consequences of Organizational Commitment." *Psychological Bulletin* 108 (2):171–94. doi:10.1037//0033-2909.108.2.171.

Maurer, T. J., and B. A. Tarulli. 1994. "Investigation of Perceived Environment, Perceived Outcome, and Person Variables in Relationship to Voluntary Development Activity by Employees." *Journal of Applied Psychology* 79 (1):3–14. doi:10.1037/0021-9010.79.1.3.

Maurer, T. J., E. M. Weiss, and F. G. Barbeite. 2003. "A Model of Involvement in Work-Related Learning and Development Activity: The Effects of Individual, Situational, Motivational and Age Variables." *Journal of Applied Psychology* 88 (4):707–24. doi:10.1037/0021-9010.88.4.707.

Meyer, J. P., and N. J. Allen. 1991. "A Three-Component Conceptualization of Organizational Commitment." *Human Resource Management Review* 1 (1):61–89. doi:10.1016/1053-4822(91)90011-Z.

Mowday, R. T., R. M. Steers, and L. W. Porter. 1979. "The Measurement of Organizational Commitment." *Journal of Vocational Behavior* 14 (2):224–47. doi:10.1016/0001-8791(79)90072-1.

OECD. 2017. *Health at a Glance 2017. OECD Indicators.* Paris: OECD Publishing. doi:10.1787/health_glance-2017-en.[Retrieved April 4, 2018]

Podsakoff, P. M., S. B. MacKenzie, J. Y. Lee, and N. P. Podsakoff. 2003. "Common Method Biases in Behavioral Research: A Critical Review of the Literature and Recommended Remedies." *Journal of Applied Psychology* 88 (5):879–903. doi:10.1037/0021-9010.88.5.879.

Super, D. E. 1957. *The Psychology of Career.* New York: Harper & Brothers.

Swailes, S. 2002. "Organizational Commitment: A Critique of the Construct and Measures." *International Journal of Management Reviews* 4 (2):155–78. doi:10.1111/1468-2370.00082.

Tikkanen, T., L. C. Lahn, A. Withnall, P. Ward, and K. Lyng. 2002. *Working Life Changes and Training of Older Workers. IV Framework Programme.* Brussels: European Commission.

Tuomi, K. and S. Vanhala. 2002. *Yrityksen Toiminta, menestyminen ja Henkilöstön Hyvinvointi. Seurantatutkimus Metalliteollisuudessa ja Vähittäiskaupan Alalla (Firm's Performance, Success and Well-Being of the Personnel. A Follow-up Study in the Metal Industry and in the Retail Sector). Studies B 40.* Helsinki: Helsinki School of Economics.

Van der Heijden, B. I. J. M. 2003. "Organisational Influences upon the Development of Occupational Expertise throughout the Career." *International Journal of Training and Development* 7 (3):142–65. doi:10.1111/1468-2419.00178.

Van der Heijden, B. I. J. M., M. J. Gorgievski, and A. H. De Lange. 2016. "Learning at the Workplace and Sustainable Employability: a Multi-source Model Moderated by Age." *European Journal of Work and Organizational Psychology* 25 (1):13–30. doi:10.1080/1359432X.2015.1007130.

Van der Heijden, B. I. J. M., A. Kümmerling, K. van Dam, E. van der Schoot, M. Estryn-Behar, and H. M. Hasselhorn. 2010. "The Impact of Social Support upon Intention to Leave among Female Nurses in Europe: Secondary Analysis of Data from the NEXT Survey." *International Journal of Nursing Studies* 47 (4):434–45. doi:10.1016/j.ijnurstu.2009.10.004.

Van der Heijden, B. I. J. M., K. van Dam, and H. M. Hasselhorn. 2009. "Intent to Leave Nursing. The Importance of Interpersonal Work Context, Work-Home Interference, and Job Satisfaction Beyond the Effect of Occupational Commitment." *Career Development International* 14 (7):616–35. doi:10.1108/13620430911005681.

Walker, A. 2005. "The Emergence of Age Management in Europe." *International Journal of Organizational Behaviour* 10 (1):685–97.

Can Sustainable HRM Reduce Work-Related Stress, Work-Family Conflict, and Burnout?

Živilė Stankevičiūtė and Asta Savanevičienė

Abstract: The effect of human resource management (HRM) on organizations and human resources is mainly explained by the perspective of mutual gain or that of conflicting outcomes. Recently, sustainable HRM is introduced as a perspective suggesting that HRM can benefit both organizations and individuals. However, sustainable HRM is still at an emerging phase. The paper defines the concept of sustainable HRM and explores the principles of sustainable HRM arguing that sustainable HRM allows reducing the negative impact of HRM on employees. Moreover, sustainable HRM fosters employee engagement in contributing to employees' well-being. The empirical findings suggest that when the principles of sustainable HRM are more clearly expressed in the organizations, employees experience less work-related stress, work-family conflict, and burnout.

The view that human resources are the most important asset of organizations has encouraged considerable interest in theory and research into the linkage between human resource management (HRM) and performance (Guest 2002, 2011). Previous studies have reported a positive effect of HRM on organizational performance (Combs et al. 2006). However, for a long time, HRM and performance linkage research showed insufficient concern for employees treating employee outcomes more as a means to an end rather than an end in themselves (Guest 2017). Only recently the literature has emphasized the need to "re-focus attention on the worker" (Guest 2002, 335) or "to focus more on employee-centered outcomes" (Van de Voorde, Paauwe, and van Veldhoven 2012, 391). In addition, two competing perspectives have explained the impact of HRM on both the organization and human resources to date. The mutual gain perspective suggests that employers and employees both benefit from HRM (Guest 1997). Hereby, conflicting outcomes perspective highlights that employers benefit most from HRM and that HRM is not beneficial and could even have a negative effect on employees in terms of their well-being (Legge 1995). Recently, a new perspective regarding the effects of HRM on organization and employees has emerged as sustainable HRM (Ehnert 2009; Mariappanadar 2014a). Sustainable HRM reflects "both/and" approach (De Prins et al. 2014) and encompasses the HRM practices that both enhance profit maximization for the organization and reduce the negative impact on employees (Mariappanadar 2003).

Certainly, previous work on HRM-performance linkage has broadened the understanding of how and why organizations achieve their goals through HRM (Jiang et al. 2012); however, HRM self-induced side effect (Ehnert 2009), or harm on employees (Mariappanadar 2014a), has largely been ignored. This disregard is reflected in employees experiencing a negative impact of HRM in terms of work-stress, burnout, and work-family conflict. According to the sixth European Working Conditions Survey (EWCS), 21% of workers are too tired after work to carry out the necessary home tasks, whereas 15% of workers worry about work when they are not working (Eurofound 2016). In 2012, according to the fifth EWSC, 22% of workers reported suffering from stress (Eurofound 2012). Employee burnout level differs from country to country; for instance, based on Gallup survey, 2.7 million German workers are feeling burned out (Nink 2015). Such a negative impact reflects on positive attitudes of employees as employee engagement. Based on 2017 trends in global employee engagement, provided by Aon Hewitt, engagement is on the decline as it dropped to 63% in 2017 comparing with 65% in 2016 (Aon Hewitt 2017).

Coping with negative consequences for employees is not only the matter of employees, but it is also in the interest of organizations. Ethical considerations have been seen as a relevant background for organizations to take responsibility for their employees (Greenwood 2013). Beside ethical issues, economic arguments gain their relevance due to growing business and society expenses in relation to harm to employees—in 2002 the European Commission calculated the cost of work-related stress at 20 billion euros a year (in the EU-15) (EU-OSHA (European Agency for Safety and Health at Work) 2014). As noted by Mariappanadar (2014b, 313), "the institutional level intervention is required to minimize the harm" created by HRM. Hereby, sustainable HRM can be used constructively to reduce employees' work-related stress, burnout, and work-family conflict. Prior research has more conceptually highlighted the role of sustainable HRM in coping with a negative impact (Mariappanadar 2012a, 2012b, 2014a, 2014b; Mariappanadar and Kramar 2014); however, the empirical testing is still lacking. This article seeks to close this gap by revealing the potential of sustainable HRM to reduce a negative impact on employees.

In the past decade, we observed an increase in publications on sustainable HRM (De Prins et al. 2014; Ehnert, Harry and Zink 2014; Harry 2014; Kramar 2014; Mariappanadar 2014a; Gollan and Xu 2014; Maley 2014; Suriyankietkaew and Avery 2014; Kozica and Kaiser 2012; Mak et al. 2014; Guerci et al. 2015; Wells 2011). To date, however, "the research on sustainable HRM is still at the pioneering if not emerging phase" (Ehnert and Harry 2012, 225). Sustainable HRM represents a new approach to people management (Clarke 2011) by identifying broader purposes for HRM and by the explicit recognition of the need to avoid negative impacts of HRM. However, prior research still struggles with key characteristics of sustainable HRM. Diverse sustainable HRM literature has provided different features of sustainable HRM (Zaugg 2009; Ehnert 2011, 2014). The article seeks to contribute to the stream of sustainable HRM research by providing the main principles of construct.

In this article we aim to disclose the main principles of sustainable HRM and to reveal the effect of sustainable HRM on employees by reducing the negative impact in terms of work-related stress, burnout, and work-family conflict. The article is based on the survey of employees working in Lithuanian organizations which are the members of Responsible Business Association of Lithuania.

This article contributes to sustainable HRM literature in several ways. First, the article introduces the principles of sustainable HRM and contributes to the answer how HRM should look like in order to deserve the sustainability attribute. Secondly, the article argues that sustainable HRM allows reducing the negative impact of HRM on employees. Thirdly, the article contributes to theory enrichment in the field of sustainable HRM. As a theoretical background for operationalizing sustainable HRM, the following three approaches have been suggested in the literature: paradox theory (Ehnert 2009), negative externality (Mariappanadar 2014a, 2014b), and stakeholder theory (Guerci and Pedrini 2014). The article contributes to the latest two streams by broadening organizational outcomes beyond the financial bottom line (stakeholder theory) and by accepting that actions of organizations that cost them less when they save can cause harm to employees (negative externality). Fourth, the article presents the empirical evidence on how sustainable HRM reduce the negative impact on employees.

This article is organized as follows. The next sections provide a theoretical foundation and develop hypotheses. The research methodology is then discussed, and the findings of the research are provided. Discussion and conclusions complete the article.

EMPLOYEES IN HRM–PERFORMANCE LINKAGE

Over the last 20 years, HRM literature highlighted the following three issues: the link between HRM and financial performance; the fit between HRM and strategy; and HRM and sustainable competitive advantage (De Prins et al. 2014). The use of human resources for achieving organization's goals has been the research mantra and reflected developments in the society and trends in the academic disciplines (Paauwe 2012). Human resource outcomes served as a key mediator between human resource management and other performance outcomes (Jiang et al. 2012; Boxall, Guthrie, and Paauwe 2016). Employees are seen more as a means to an end rather than an end in themselves (Guest 2017). The idea that employees *per se* are of the high relevance has largely been ignored. Moreover, in the mainstream literature, the unitarist approach has prevailed. According to the mutual gain perspective, employees and employers both benefit from HRM. In the pluralistic approach, conflicting goals and interests of both parties are acknowledged. Hereby, the conflict outcomes perspective sees HRM as an exploitative in nature (Legge 1995) and underlines that HRM is not beneficial or may even be harmful for employees (Van De vorde, Paauwe, and van Veldhoven 2012).

Research into the negative effect of HRM on employees presents a variety of negative consequences. A number of studies focus on a separate negative impact such as work-related stress, work-family conflict (Bolino and Turnley 2005), and burnout (Kroon, van de Voorde, and van Veldhoven 2009). Other studies treat a negative impact as a part of employee well-being under the umbrella of health-related well-being (Grant, Christianson, and Price 2007) or based on the Job Demands-Resources model (JD-R model) introduced by Demerouti et al. (2001).

By managing the negative impact on employees, organizations should also address the positive outcomes such as employee engagement. Establishing employee engagement is a crucial goal of HRM since it predicts employee outcomes and organizational financial performance (Saks 2006). Engagement has positive implications at individual and collective levels. On an individual level engagement can boost performance, creativity while preventing absence from work. On a collective level engagement is positively related to commitment to the organization, client satisfaction, and employee retention (Eurofound 2016). In general, employee engagement reflects a positive attitude, meanwhile work-related stress, work-family conflict, and burnout reflect a negative side of employee well-being.

The necessity to cope with a negative impact on employees is well established in the literature, as harm on employees harm the performance (Guest 2017). Stress at work seems to be a major cost to organizations and countries in a wider sense, "as it affects productivity, notably through absenteeism and presenteeism (i.e., the practice of attending work even when employees feel too ill to be able to work effectively)" (European foundation for the improvement of living and working conditions, 2010, 2). For instance, the Sainsbury Centre of Mental Health in 2007 estimated that sickness absence due to depression, anxiety, and stress cost British society approx. £1.26 billion a year (European Foundation for the Improvement of Living and Working Conditions, 2010). Striving for better performance means that organizations focus on challenges to reframe HRM. Mariappanadar (2014b) suggests changes at the institutional level through application of a new approach to HRM, namely sustainable HRM.

SUSTAINABLE HRM FOR REDUCING A NEGATIVE IMPACT ON EMPLOYEES

Sustainable HRM

Generally speaking, sustainable HRM offers an alternative approach to people management (Clarke 2011). It can be considered as an extension of strategic HRM focusing on multiple bottom lines ("triple-bottom line"), i.e., economic, social, and environmental organizational performance (Guerci, Shani, and Solari 2014). The diverse literature on sustainable HRM provides several definitions for the construct; however, one of the most cited is the following definition by Ehnert (2009, 74):

> Sustainable HRM is the pattern of planned or emerging human resource strategies and practices intended to enable organisational goal achievement while simultaneously reproducing the HR base over a long-lasting calendar time and controlling for self-induced side and feedback effects of HR systems on the HR base and thus on the company itself."

According to Ehnert (2006, 14), one of the main objectives of sustainable HRM is "to evaluate and assess negative effects of HR activities on the HR base and on the sources for

HR." Recently, Kramar (2014, 1084) has expanded the definition of Ehnert (2009) distinctly highlighting that sustainable HRM "seeks to minimise the negative impacts on . . . people and communities . . ." The capacity of sustainable HRM to reduce the negative impact on employees is the core idea in the works of Mariappanadar (2003, 2012a, 2012b, 2014a, 2014b). Mariappanadar (2014b) emphasizes the synthesis effect of sustainable HRM where the organizations can improve organizational outcomes through HRM as well as reduce the harm of HRM on employees, because two polarities (financial outcomes and employee well-being) are not mutually exclusive, but they are mutually reinforcing (Mariappanadar and Kramar 2014). In addition, the theory of negative externality can be employed for operationalizing sustainable HRM and explaining its value for business. Externality is "something that, while it does not monetarily affect the company that produces goods, does harm the living standard of society as a whole" (Mariappanadar 2014b, 315). Negative externality is something that costs the organization less for their actions than they save, but these actions can have a negative impact on employees and on the whole society. Moreover, social costs are imposed on the weaker section on the society (Mariappanadar 2014b). However, in a long-term perspective, organizations will also sustain the loss. For instance, high-performance work systems result in work intensification that in turn causes stress (Jensen, Patel, and Messersmith 2013). At the individual level, stress may be related to increased medical costs and reduced income. At the organizational level, the financial implications of work-related stress are associated with deterioration of productivity, higher levels of absenteeism, and employee turnover (European Agency for Safety and Health at Work) 2014). In similar situations "win-win" status is possible when employing sustainable HRM as it refers to maintaining, renewing, and restoring human resources (Clarke 2011), reducing the harm on employees, and enhancing profit for the organization (Mariappanadar 2014a). However, the diverse literature on sustainable HRM still searches for an answer concerning the main features of the construct.

The Principles of Sustainable HRM

The principles of sustainable HRM explain how sustainability can be used for HRM. The principles describe how HRM should look like in order to deserve the attribute "sustainable." Literature review allows us to state that there is the lack of implicitly and/or explicitly expressed principles of sustainable HRM (Zaugg, Blum, and Thom 2001; Ehnert 2011; De Prins et al. 2014; Järlström, Saru, and Vanhala 2018). However, based on mentioned research, some general principles of sustainable HRM such as long-term orientation, preservation of human resources, environmental protection, participation of employees, employee as an equal partner, cooperation between employees, development of employees' potential, flexibility, fairness and equal opportunities, could be formulated. These principles fall into five clusters, namely employee competencies, voice of employees, employee-employer relations, care of employees, and care of environment.

Employee competencies cluster covers two principles, i.e., development of employees' potential and long-term orientation. Development of employees' potential means that it is necessary, but not sufficient to development competencies the employees need now, it is relevant to identifying and developing future skills and capabilities. Long-term orientation is reflected in human resource planning (labor market analysis and forecast (Zaugg et al. 2001); in "future opportunity" job description (Becker and Smith 2013); and in human resource attraction and recruiting (Harry 2014).

Voice of employees cluster includes one principle, i.e., participation of employees. From the sustainable HRM point of view, participation of employees reflects the conditions that the organization creates for employees to provide proposals for improvement of organization's activities, to receive information, and to participate in decision making.

Employee-employer relations cluster covers the following three principles: employee as an equal partner, cooperation between employees, and fairness and equal opportunities. The principle of employee as an equal partner is directly related to the stakeholder perspective treating employee as one of main stakeholders (Zink 2007; Guerci et al. 2014). Fairness and equal opportunities are largely discussed in the field of ethical HRM (Greenwood 2002; Rowan 2000). From the sustainable HRM point of view, procedural fairness of selection, performance evaluation, and compensation systems are of high importance. Employees' rights to receive fair pay and to receive the same pay for the same job are the keystones of sustainable HRM. Equal opportunities reflect the employment and work organization processes, when the changes in employees' status are not based on socio-demographic characteristics of these employees. Cooperation between employees allows assessing the nature of relations between employees; it includes not only relations between employees, but also relations between employees and managers.

Care of employees cluster covers two principles, i.e., preservation of employees and flexibility. According to Ehnert (2009), the organization needs to ensure that it will maintain healthy and productive labor force. The preservation of human resources allows assessing how much effort directed towards maintaining of the employees and their reproduction (regeneration) is made by the organization; it is related to professional health management (Docherty, Kira, and Shani 2009; Pfeffer 2010; Zink 2014), reconciliation of work and personal life (Rowan 2000; Zaugg et al. 2001), reduction of stress, payment of reasonable minimum salary (Rowan 2000), and balance of workload (Mariappanadar 2012a, 2012b; Pfeffer 2010).

The flexibility debate tends to concentrate on the notions of functional and numerical flexibility. Functional flexibility is usually seen as the ability to respond to changes in business needs by having multi-skilled, adaptable, and internally mobile employees; hereby, numerical flexibility is the ability of the organization to vary the quantity of work force employed to match changes in the business needs (Carvalho and Cabral-Cardoso 2008). From the sustainable HRM point of view, flexibility is related to the nature of work organization. It includes rotation of employees, substitution of employees, and flexible work schedule, which allows matching the interests of employer and employee.

Care of environment includes the principle of environmental protection. As sustainability integrates economic, social, and environmental bottom lines, sustainable HRM should also incorporate environmental dimension. Environmental protection is related to environmentally friendly working conditions, the alternatives for commuting, the training of environmental protection, and the interconnection between environmental protection and some HRM functions such as performance management and pay for performance.

Work-Related Stress, Burnout, and Work-Family Conflict as Negative Outcomes on Employees

As it was mentioned before, the negative impact of HRM on employees can occur in a variety of forms. In this article, the focus is on three constructs: work-related stress, burnout, and work-family conflict.

Work-Related Stress

According to the European Commission (European Commission 2011, 12), stress is "a state, which is accompanied by physical, psychological or social complaints or dysfunctions and which results from individuals feeling unable to bridge a gap with the requirements or expectations placed on them." As stated by Ongori and Agolla (2008), work-related stress is defined as the perception of a discrepancy between environmental demands (stressors) and individual capacities to fulfill these demands.

Work-related stress is treated as a structural problem that exerts an individual effect on each employee and influences the entire performance of an organization. According to Ongori and Agolla (2008), the cost of work-related stress is very high in many organizations; meanwhile the European Commission underlines that work stress may reduce effectiveness at work and may cause ill health (European Commission 2011). European Framework Agreement on Work-Related Stress (2014) states that stress-related problems include high absenteeism, high turnover, complaints by workers, or interpersonal conflicts.

Based on the empirical data, Macky and Boxall (2008) conclude that work intensity and a high-performance work system cause more stress. According to Kira and Lifvergren (2014), the consumption of human resources results in stress and hereby decreases employee capabilities to function and adapt. Mariappanadar (2012b) argues that employees who feel stress tend to use sick leave as a stress coping strategy to recuperate from illness, and emphasizes the influence of stress on employee's private life. European Framework Agreement on Work-Related Stress (2014) provides a list of factors which can cause stress, namely, work organization and processes (e.g., working time arrangements, workload, match between employee's skills and job requirements); communication (e.g., uncertainty about what is expected at work, employment prospects); working conditions and environment; subjective factors (e.g., perceived lack of support from managers and coworkers). Such principles of sustainable HRM as long-term orientation, preservation of human resources, development of employees' potential, flexibility, participation of employee, employer as an equal partner, and cooperation between employees are directed at reducing the factors which cause work-related stress. Accordingly, sustainable HRM (and clusters of sustainable HRM principles) should be negatively related to work-related stress:

H1. When sustainable HRM is more clearly expressed, the employees' work-related stress decreases.

Work-Family Conflict

Work-family conflict could be defined as "a form of inter-role conflict in which the role pressures from the work and family domains are mutually incompatible in some respect" (Greenhaus and Beutell 1985, 77).

Role theory is one of the most popular theoretical perspectives that explains the construct of work-family conflict and its antecedents (Bolino and Turnley 2005; Bakar and Salleh 2015). The employees will increasingly be unable to handle each role successfully if they take multiple roles, which in the long-term leads to the role conflict. Employees focus on difficulties to perform roles due to limited resources (time and energy) or due to incompatibility between different roles (Bakar and Salleh 2015). Greenhaus and Beutell (1985) present a model by identifying the following three forms of work-family conflict: time-based conflict; strain-based conflict, and behavior-based conflict. From work domain perspective, time-based conflict is consistent with worked hours, inflexible work schedule, or shiftwork. Strain-based conflict is expressed by role ambiguity or conflict. Therefore, behavior-based conflict relies on expectations for secretiveness. Byron (2005) supports three types of antecedents of work-family conflict: work domain variables, non-work domain variables, and individual and demographic variables. Work domain variables consider the effect of job and workplace factors such as schedule flexibility, work support, work involvement, or hours spend at work. Clearly, among the factors that cause work-family conflict are the factors that do not fit the context of sustainable HRM. Accordingly, sustainable HRM (and clusters of sustainable HRM principles) should be negatively related to work-family conflict.

H2. When sustainable HRM is more clearly expressed, the employees' work-family conflict decreases.

Burnout

Burnout is a metaphor that is commonly used to describe a state of mental weariness (Schaufeli and Bakker 2004). Burnout is more than stress. It is a prolonged exposure to stress (Jamil, Raja, and Darr 2013). Burnout has been commonly linked to absenteeism and turnover (Jamil et al. 2013). According to Kira and Lifvergren (2014), the consumption of human resources results in burnout and therefore decreases employees' capabilities to act and adapt. Burnout researchers define engagement as the opposite or positive antithesis of burnout. According to Maslach, Schaufeli, and Leiter (2001), engagement is characterized by energy, involvement, and efficacy, the direct opposite of the three burnout dimensions of exhaustion, cynicism, and inefficacy. Exhaustion refers to fatigue but does not make a direct reference to other people as the source of those feelings; cynicism reflects indifference or a distant attitude toward work in general; professional efficacy encompasses social and nonsocial aspects of occupational accomplishments (Schaufeli et al. 2002; Schaufeli, Leiter, and

Maslach 2009). Relevant and typical antecedents of burnout include factors such as lack of social support, lack of mutual working relationships, lack of participation in decision making, lack of organizational trust, lack of feedback, and work or role overload (Jamil et al. 2013). Sustainable HRM is on the opposite side of the mentioned antecedents. Accordingly, sustainable HRM (and clusters of sustainable HRM principles) should be negatively related to burnout.

H3. When sustainable HRM is more clearly expressed, the employees' burnout decreases.

RESEARCH METHODOLOGY

Sample

Data was collected between May and June 2015 by means of the paper questionnaire. It was distributed to the employees of nine organizations that are the members of Responsible Business Association of Lithuania (nine organizations accepted the invitation to take part in the research). The reason for choosing the organizations of the Association was the assumption that they had a deeper knowledge of sustainability and that their activities would provide and confirm the evidence that the principles of sustainable HRM reduce the negative impact on employees.

At the end of quantitative research, 383 questionnaires were collected, and 375 were suitable for the research.

Questionnaire and Measures

Because no scale could be found in literature for sustainable HRM, the items were developed following the scientific literature linking sustainability and HRM (Ehnert 2009, 2014; Zaugg 2009; De Prins et al. 2014) and were based on the conceptualization of the sustainable HRM principles discussed in that article. For measuring the negative impact on the employees (outcomes), scales provided in the literature were used.

The survey consisted of 14 parts, divided into three main sections, and it included a short cover letter that explained the purpose of the study. The first section was to determine the extent to which the respondents assess each of the nine principles of sustainable HRM. The second section aimed to reveal the negative impact on employees; while the third section analyzed employees' demography.

The principles of sustainable HRM. The construct of sustainable HRM comprised the following nine subscales: long-term orientation (four items, Cronbach's alpha −0.784); preservation of human resources (five items, Cronbach's alpha −0.607); environmental protection five items, Cronbach's alpha −0.746); participation of employees (five items, Cronbach's alpha −0.797); employee as an equal partner (four items, Cronbach's alpha −0.719); cooperation between employees (six items, Cronbach's alpha −0.809); development of employees' potential (six items, Cronbach's alpha −0.859); flexibility (two items, Cronbach's alpha

-0.535); and fairness and equal opportunities (seven items, Cronbach's alpha −0.866). The items of each subscale were measured on a scale ranging from 1 (totally disagree) to 4 (totally agree); the possibility to choose "I don't know/I can't answer" was included. However, for the sake of clarity, the principles were combined into five clusters according to the logical argumentation provided in the theoretical part.

Work-related stress. It was measured with a nine-scale shortened version of the Job Stress Scale developed by Parker and Decotiis (1983) and used by Jamal and Baba (1992) (as cited in Fields 2002). Cronbach's alpha for the scale was 0.869.

Work-family conflict. Work-family conflict was measured using an eight-item scale. The scale was based on items developed by Kopelman, Greenhaus, and Connolly (1983) (as cited in Fields 2002). Cronbach's alpha for the scale was 0.911.

Burnout. Burnout was measured with a 15-item scale developed by Schauffeli et al. (2002. Cronbach's alpha for the scale was 0.860.

Responses for all three constructs were made on a 5-point scale ranging from 1 (totally disagree) to 5 (totally agree).

Control variables. Age, gender, education, position (managerial or not), and working period in the organization were used as control variables in all of the analyses.

RESULTS

The means, standard deviations for the scales, and a correlation matrix are provided in Table 1. For condensation reasons, the results are provided based on principle clusters, not on separate principles.

Bivariate correlations were examined in order to determine the associations between clusters of the principles of sustainable HRM and each construct of the negative impact on employees.

Work-related stress was negatively related to each cluster of sustainable HRM principles, except for care of environment. However, the relationship is weak ($r < 0.2$–0.4) (Burns 2000). Work-related stress statistically has the most significant negative correlation with employee-employer relations ($r = -0.293$, $p < 0.01$) and a less significant one with employee competencies ($r = -0.211$, $p < 0.01$). A similar situation was noticed regarding the work-family conflict correlation with principle clusters. Work-family conflict statistically has the most significant negative correlation with care of employees ($r = -0.297$, $p < 0.01$) and less significant one with employee competencies ($r = -0.244$, $p < 0.01$). A slightly different situation was identified in the case of burnout, because all clusters correlate with the mentioned construct. Statistically burnout was most significantly related to the participation of employees ($r = -0.430$, $p < 0.01$) and less significantly with environmental protection ($r = -0.201$, $p < 0.01$).

Hierarchical regression was used to test hypotheses (Table 2). Step 1 includes the control variables, Step 2 includes the clusters of sustainable HRM principles, and Step 3 includes sustainable HRM. For work-related stress (-0.124, $p < 0.05$), work-family conflict (-0.103, $p < 0.1$), and burnout (-0.216, $p < 0.001$) negative relationships were found with sustainable

TABLE 1

Means, Standard Deviations and Correlations

Variable	M	SD	1	2	3	4	5	6	7	8	9	10	11	12	13	14
1 Age	2.93	1.15	—													
2 Education	2.18	1.73	0.080													
3 Position	1.83	0.37	−0.159**	0.229**												
4 Work duration	2.46	0.90	0.520**	−0.022	−0.181**											
5 Gender	1.67	0.47	0.067	0.056	0.003	0.017										
6 Employee competencies			0.085	−0.123*	−0.196*	0.097	0.072									
7 Care of employees			0.037	−0.227**	−0.133*	0.057	0.025	0.410**								
8 Employee-employer relations			−0.007	−0.221**	−0.138**	−0.022	0.071	0.651**	0.456**							
9 Vioce of employees	2.97	0.58	0.039	−0.183**	−0.167**	0.022	0.092	0.504**	0.335**	0.564**						
10 Care of environment	2.98	0.63	0.194**	0.147*	−0.186**	0.098	−0.041	0.366**	0.212**	0.325**	0.739**					
11 Sustainable HRM	2.55	0.48	0.010	−0.276**	−0.284**	0.142	−0.131	0.461**	0.303**	0.490**	0.813**	0.616**				
12 Work-related stress	3.04	0.48	0.055	0.124*	0.109*	0.047	0.079	−0.211**	−0.281**	−0.293**	−0.226**	−0.113	−0.297**			
13 Work-family conflict	2.83	0.42	−0.055	0.095	0.135*	0.021	0.080	−0.244**	−0.297**	−0.292**	−0.277**	−0.125	−0.312**	0.744**		
14 Burnout	2.60	0.48	−0.126*	0.116*	0.196**	−0.021	−0.064	−0.373**	−0.383**	−0.397**	−0.430**	−0.201**	−0.441**	0.590**	0.607**	

$**p < 0.01$; $*p < 0.05$.

TABLE 2
Regression Analysis

| | Dependent variables | | | | | | | | |
| | Work-related stress | | | Work-family conflict | | | Burnout | | |
	Step 1	Step 2	Step 3	Step 1	Step 2	Step 3	Step 1	Step 2	Step 3
Control variables									
Age	0.005	0.004	−0.001	−0.088	−101*	−0.094	−0.095	−0.103*	−0.108*
Education	0.026	−0.045	0.018	0.005	−0.087*	−0.002	0.035	−0.043	0.024
Position	0.118**	0.066	0.100*	0.115**	0.066	0.101*	0.194***	0.101**	0.162*
Work duration	0.052	0.052	0.066	0.091	0.102*	0.103	0.054	0.070	0.080
Gender	0.105*	0.131**	0.104**	0.075	0.119**	0.074	−0.022	0.024	−0.026
Independent variables (clusters of principles)									
Employee competencies		0.046			0.014			−0.028	
Care of employees		−0.189***			−0.230****			−0.214****	
Employee-employer relations		−0.258***			−0.242***			−0.203***	
Voice of employees		−0.022			−0.079			−0.210***	
Care of environment		0.066			0.143			0.089	
Independent variables									
Sustainable HRM			−0.124**			−0.103*			−0.216****
F[a]	1.933*	5.449****	2.497**	1.777	7.504****	2.087*	3.604***	13.276****	5.908****
Overall R^2	0.028	0.141	0.043	0.025	0.182	0.035	0.051	0.285	0.095
Adjusted R^2	0.013	0.115	0.026	0.011	0.158	0.018	0.037	0.264	0.079
Change in adjusted R^2	0.013	0.102	0.013	0.011	0.147	0.010	0.037	0.227	0.042

Step 1 degrees of freedom 5. Step 2 degrees of freedom 10. Step 2 degrees of freedom 6.

[a] Step 1 degrees of freedom 5. Step 2 degrees of freedom 10. Step 2 degrees of freedom 6.
$*p < 0.1$; $**p < 0.05$; $***p < 0.01$; $****p < 0.001$.

HRM. This means that hypotheses H1, H2, and H3 were supported. However, as it is seen from Table 2, not all clusters of principles are statistically significant in relation to negative impact on employees. Employees work-related stress would decrease if the care of employees and employer-employee relations were perceived by employees as increased. The results for work-family conflict are essentially the same. In case of burnout, besides the care of employees and employer-employee relations, participation of employees was perceived as a tool for reducing a prolonged exposure to stress (Jamil et al. 2013). This leads to the idea that in the case of sustainable HRM a bundle of principles rather than separate principles plays an important role in reducing the negative impact on employees in forms of work-related stress, work-family conflict, and burnout.

DISCUSSION

This article examined the possibility that engaging employees in sustainable HRM could positively affect them by reducing the negative impact. The discussion section is organized as follows: firstly, discussion on theoretical contribution is presented; then the discussion is based on empirical findings.

The imperative for business to cope with a negative impact of HRM on employees has not only ethical, but also economic arguments behind itself. It is relevant to recognize that a negative impact on employees imposes negative consequences on the organization and on the society. At the individual level, work-related stress may be related to medical cost and reduced income. At the organizational level, the financial implications of work-related stress are associated with a higher level of absenteeism, employee turnover, and lower quality productivity. At the society level, work-related stress can reduce economic productivity and strain national health system (European Agency for Safety and Health at Work) 2014). As stated by Garton (2017), the psychological and physical problems of burned-out employees, which cost an estimated $125 billion to $190 billion a year in healthcare spending in the United States, are the most obvious. However, high turnover, low productivity, and the loss of the most capable talent are the true cost to each organization. Bakker, van Emmerik, and van Riet (2008) showed that burnout was associated with subsequent poorer performance. In contrast, research on employee engagement was associated with positive performance-related outcomes (Schaufeli et al. 2009).

That situation leads the researchers and practitioners to search for the way of reducing such a negative impact. Recently, sustainable HRM has been introduced as an alternative approach for people management. As "human beings are in the centre of concern for sustainable development" (UNCED (United Nations Conference on environment and development) 1992, 2), sustainable HRM underlines the relevance of employees. Accordingly, sustainable HRM could be implemented for coping with a negative impact on employees.

In this article, the understanding of sustainable HRM is in accord with "triple bottom line" approach, and it explicitly underlines the environmental aspects in contrast to Zaugg et al. (2001) or Thom and Zaugg (2004). In line with stakeholder theory (Guerci and Pedrini 2014) and the theory of negative externality (Mariappanadar 2012a, 2012b), sustainable HRM addresses the negative impact of HRM on employees and the necessity to reduce it while striving to maintain, develop, and regenerate the labor force. The article conceptualizes the principles of sustainable HTM based on the characteristics provided in previous work, and hereby contributes to literature by taking a broader view in understanding how HRM should look like in order to deserve an attribute "sustainable."

Given that sustainable HRM is expressed via increased employee competencies, positive employee-employer relationships, care of employees, care of environment, and voice of employees, the article theoretically supports the possibility for organizations to reduce the negative impact on employees. Consistent with the hypotheses, the empirical findings indicate that sustainable HRM reduces the negative impact on employees.

The findings demonstrate that when the care of employees is more clearly expressed, employees feel less job stress and burnout, which is also true about the principle of flexibility that represents one principle of the cluster, i.e., care of employees. These findings are in line with the research of Grzywacz, Carlson, and Shulkin (2008), i.e., employees working flextime or compressed workweeks experience less stress and burnout. However, these results are in contrast with the results of Mariappanadar and Kramar (2014) who argue that teleworking and compressed working week have a negative impact on employees (the level of absenteeism and sick leave is increasing). The sixth EWCS (Eurofound 2016) reported that workers working long hours are more likely to have problems with work-life balance (62%). Olsen and Dahl (2010), based on research in Norway, concluded that flexibility in the work schedule when working regular hours had no effect on the work-family balance. These findings are related to findings of the article, as when the flexibility increases, the work-family conflict decreases.

Although the empirical results on different aspects of flexibility differ, business is in need to adopt the best practices in order to reduce work-life conflict. The possibility of taking time off during working hours is one of good examples already implemented in a huge amount of organizations. According to the sixth EWCS (Eurofound 2016), overall 66% of workers in the EU28 reported that arranging to take an hour or two off during working time to take care of personal matters is quite easy (fairly or very easy).

Macky and Boxall (2008) highlight that the development of employees' potential does not increase the work-family conflict and work-related stress. Harry (2014) argues for relations between sustainability and people development: sustainability requires more attention to human resource development and increasing competencies as many organizations have discovered that severely cutting down on training and development, even during economic crises, creates longer-term problems (Harry 2014). However, according the research results, no significant relation were found between employee competencies and negative impact on employees. That could be explained by high education level of Lithuanians.

The empirical study revealed that the mean rank of the principle of environmental protection is lowest among other principles. This could mean that the organizations do not put effort to embed environmental policies and actions into organizations. Jackson and Seo (2010) claim that the influence of environmental imperatives should be visible across all aspects of HRM. According to Dubois and Dubois (2012), introducing environmental strategy requires changes in thinking and behavior across all levels of employees. The study results support the idea of Dubois and Dubois (2012) concerning the necessity to change employees thinking or even mentality, as based on the study results there are no statistically significant correlations between the principle of environmental protection and work-related stress and work-family conflict.

In general, the empirical results indicate that when the principles of sustainable HRM are more clearly expressed, employees experience less work-related stress, work-family conflict, and burnout. These results correspond to theoretical insights concerning the principles of sustainable HRM impact on employees by reducing the negative impact (Mariappanadar 2014a, 2014b). Hereby, the pool of empirical evidence that sustainable HRM can be used in order to reduce the negative HRM on employees is expanded.

CONCLUSIONS AND LIMITATIONS

This article sheds light on the necessity to cope with a negative impact on employees as negative effects impose a significant burden (also financial) on individuals, organizations, and society in the long-term perspective. The article focuses on sustainable HRM, its main principles, and on empirical evidence how the principles of sustainable HRM reduce the negative impact of HRM on employees in the form of work-related stress, burnout, and work-family conflict.

From the theoretical point of view, some conclusions could be drawn. Starting from discussion on the place of an employee in the HRM-performance linkage, the article follows the pluralistic approach, where conflicting goals of employees and employers are acknowledged. The duality of the impact of HRM on employees is revealed identifying a positive (such as engagement) and a negative (such as work-related stress, burnout, work-family conflict) impact and the objective to minimize the negative impact. Following "triple-bottom line" approach, the article supports sustainable HRM for reducing the negative impact on employees. Trying to contribute to the theoretical and practical discussion on the features of sustainable HRM, the principles and the cluster of sustainable HRM principles are revealed. Sustainable HRM encompasses employee competencies, employee-employer relationships, care of employees, care of environment and voice of employees which add value to complex understanding of sustainable HRM

From the empirical point of view, the article responds to Ehnert et al.'s (2014) claim that the research should be conducted in the organizations and the data should not be taken from the social responsibility reports. In terms of work-related stress (-0.214, $p < 0.05$), work-family conflict (-0.203, $p < 0.1$), and burnout (-0.216, $p < 0.001$), negative relationships were found with sustainable HRM. This means that hypotheses H1, H2, and H3 were supported. However, only some clusters of principles are statistically significant in relation to negative outcomes. This leads to the idea that in sustainable HRM a bundle of principles rather than separate principles plays an important role in reducing the negative impact on employees in the forms of work-related stress, work-family conflict, and burnout.

The research has implications for practitioners. The analysis revealed that sustainable HRM can lead to lower degree of work-related stress, burnout, and work-family conflict.

Therefore, the organizations should carefully manage the employees' competencies and devote time and financial resources to their development. Business needs to take care of employees by arranging flexibility in HRM. Organizations are encouraged to treat employees as equal partners, to enhance employee cooperation, or to scrutinize and manage practices related to fairness and equal opportunities. However, some caution for organizations could be provided. Given that the implementation of sustainable HRM can be influenced by many factors, variations in the principles of sustainable HRM across organizations cannot be avoided, which will lead to different results in terms of reducing the negative impact and enhancing employee engagement. However, the finding is empirical evidence that sustainable HRM pays off, i.e., the organizations seeking to reduce work-related stress, work-family conflict, and burnout can use the principles of sustainable HRM as a managerial framework.

The study has several limitations that need to be mentioned. The first limitation is the narrow data source: all data were collected from the employees working in the organizations that are the members of Responsible Business Association of Lithuania. That fact might have reduced variation among responses, suggesting the need for caution with generalizations. With more employees working in different industries, future studies will overcome this limitation. The second limitation is research level. The empirical research is limited to the impact of sustainable HRM principles on the individual level, and organizations' financial performance is not assessed. Hereby, the "synthesis effect" is not truly tested. Future studies will overcome this limitation through investigating the impact of sustainable HRM principles not only on employees, but also on organizational performance such as financial performance.

ACKNOWLEDGMENTS

The authors thank EIASM for organizing the Workshop for Strategic Human Resource Management that provided the opportunity to engage in this discussion. We also thank the French Investissements d'Avenir (ANR-11-IDEX-0003/Labex Ecodec/ANR-11-LABX-0047) for funding our working meetings to produce this article. Additionally, we thank HEC Paris School of Management and NEOMA Business School for their support of our research.

REFERENCES

AON Hewitt. 2017. *2017 Trends in Global Employee Engagement.* http://www.modernsurvey.com/wp-content/uploads/2017/04/2017-Trends-in-Global-Employee-Engagement.pdf

Bakar, Z. A., and R. Salleh. 2015. "Role Demands, Work-Family Conflict and Motivation: A Proposed Framework." *Global Business and Management Research: An International Journal* 7 (2):78–87.

Bakker, A. B., H. Van Emmerik, and P. Van Riet. 2008. "How Job Demands, Resources, and Burnout Predict Objective Performance: A Constructive Replication." *Anxiety, Stress, and Coping* 21 (3):309–24.

Becker, W. S., and R. Smith. 2013. "Social and Environmental Responsibility, Sustainability, and Human Resource Practices." In *Sustainable Value Chain Management: A Research Anthology*, edited by A. Lindgreen, F. Maon, J. Vanhamme, and S. Sen, 153–65. Gower Publications.

Bolino, M. C., and W. H. Turnley. 2005. "The Personal Costs of Citizenship Behavior: The Relationship between Individual Initiative and Role Overload, Job Stress, and Work-Family Conflict." *Journal of Applied Psychology* 90 (4):740–8. doi:10.1037/0021-9010.90.4.740.

Boxall, P., J. P. Guthrie, and J. Paauwe. 2016. "Editorial Introduction: Progressing Our Understanding of the Mediating Variables Linking HRM, Employee Well-Being and Organisational Performance." *Human Resource Management Journal* 26 (2):103–11. doi:10.1111/1748-8583.12104.

Burns, R. B. 2000. *Introduction to Research Methods.* (4th ed.). London: Sage Publications.

Byron, K. 2005. "A Meta-Analytic Review of Work–Family Conflict and Its Antecedents." *Journal of Vocational Behavior* 67 (2):169–98. doi:10.1016/j.jvb.2004.08.009.

Carvalho, A., and C. Cabral-Cardoso. 2008. "Flexibility through HRM in Management Consulting Firms." *Personnel Review* 37 (3):332–49. doi:10.1108/00483480810862305.

Clarke, M. 2011. "Sustainable HRM: a New Approach to People Management". In *Readings in HRM and Sustainability*, edited by M. Clarke, 1–6. Prahran: Tilde University Press.

Combs, J., Y. Liu, A. Hall, and D. Ketchen. 2006. "How Much Do High-performance Work Practices Matter? A Meta-analysis of Their Effects on Organizational Performance." *Personnel Psychology* 59 (3):501–28. doi: 10.1111/j.1744-6570.2006.00045.x.

De Prins, P., L. Van Beirendonck, A. De Vos, and J. Segers. 2014. "Sustainable HRM. Bridging Theory and Practice Trough the respect Openness Continuity (ROC)-Model." *Management Review* 25 (4):244–84.

Demerouti, E., A. B. Bakker, F. Nachreiner, and W. B. Schaufeli. 2001. "The Job Demands-Resources Model of Burnout." *Journal of Applied Psychology* 86 (3):499–512. doi:10.1037/0021-9010.86.3.499.

Docherty, P., M. Kira, and A. B.(Rami) Shani. 2009. "What the World Needs Now is Sustainable Work Systems." In *Creating Sustainable Work Systems*, edited by P. Docherty, M. Kira, and A.B.(Rami) Shani, 1–21. London: Routledge.

Dubois, C. L. Z., and D. A. Dubois. 2012. "Strategic HRM as Social Design for Environmental Sustainability in Organization." *Human Resource Management* 51 (6):799–826. doi:10.1002/hrm.21504.

Ehnert, I. 2006. *Sustainability Issues in Human Resource Management: Linkages, Theoretical Approaches, and Outlines for an Emerging Field*. Aston, Birmingham: Paper prepared for 21st EIASM SHRM Workshop.

Ehnert, I. 2009. *Sustainable Human Resource Management: A Conceptual and Exploratory Analysis from a Paradox Perspective*. Heidelberg: Physica-Verlag.

Ehnert, I. 2011. Sustainability and Human Resource Management: a Model and Suggestions for Future Research. In *The Future of Employment Relations*, edited by A. Wilkinson, and K. Townsend, 215–37. Palgrave.

Ehnert, I. 2014. "Paradox as a Lens for Theorizing Sustainable HRM." In *Sustainability and Human Resource Management. Developing Sustainable Business Organizations*, edited by I. Ehnert, W. Harry, and K. J. Zink, 247–71. Berlin Heidelberg: Springer.

Ehnert, I., and W. Harry. 2012. "Recent Developments and Future Prospects on Sustainable Human Resource Management: Introduction to the Special Issue." *Management Revu* 23 (3):221–38. doi:10.5771/0935-9915-2012-3-221.

Ehnert, I., W. Harry, and K. J. Zink. 2014. "Sustainability and HRM." In *Sustainability and Human Resource Management. Developing Sustainable Business Organizations*, edited by I. Ehnert, W. Harry, and K. J. Zink, 3–32. Berlin Heidelberg: Springer.

EU-OSHA (European Agency for Safety and Health at Work). 2014. *Calculating the Cost of Work-Related Stress and Psychosocial Risks*. Luxembourg: Publications Office of the European Union.

Eurofound. 2012. *Fifth European Working Conditions Survey*. Luxembourg: Publications Office of the European Union.

Eurofound. 2016. *Sixth European Working Conditions Survey – Overview Report*. Luxembourg: Publications office of the European Union.

European Commission. 2011. Report on the Implementation of the European Social Partners' Framework Agreement on Work-related Stress. http://erc-online.eu/wp-content/uploads/2015/03/COM_SEC20110241_EN.pdf

European Foundation for the Improvement of Living and Working Conditions. 2010. Work related stress. https://www.eurofound.europa.eu/sites/default/files/ef_files/docs/ewco/tn1004059s/tn1004059s.pdf

European Framework Agreement on Work-Related Stress. 2014. https://osha.europa.eu/en/legislation/guidelines/framework-agreement-on-work-related-stress

Fields, D. L. 2002. *Taking the Measure of Work. A Guide to Validated Scales for Organizational Research and Diagnosis*. Thousands Oaks: Sage Publications.

Garton, E. 2017. "Employee Burnout is a Problem with the company, not the Person." *Harward Business Review*.

Gollan, P. J., and Y. Xu. 2014. "Fostering Corporate Sustainability. Sustainability and HRM." In *Sustainability and Human Resource Management. Developing Sustainable Business Organizations*, edited by I. Ehnert, W. Harry, and K. J. Zink, 225–45. Berlin Heidelberg: Springer.

Grant, A. M., M. K. Christianson, and R. H. Price. 2007. "Happiness, Health, or Relationships? Managerial Practices and Employee Well-Being Tradeoffs." *Academy of Management Perspectives* 21 (3):51–63. doi: 10.5465/amp.2007.26421238.

Greenhaus, J. H., and N. J. Beutell. 1985. "Sources of Conflict between Work and Family Roles." *Academy of Management Review* 10 (1):76–88. doi:10.5465/amr.1985.4277352.

Greenwood, M. 2013. "Ethical Analyses of HRM: A Review and Research Agenda." *Journal of Business Ethics* 114 (2):355–66. doi:10.1007/s10551-012-1354-y.

Greenwood, M. R. 2002. "Ethics and HRM: a Review and Conceptual Analysis." *Journal of Business Ethics* 36 (3): 261–78. doi:10.1023/A:1014090411946.

Grzywacz, J. G., D. S. Carlson, and S. Shulkin. 2008. "Schedule Flexibility and Stress: Linking Formal Flexible Arrangements and Perceived Flexibility to Employee Health." *Community, Work and Family* 11 (2):199–214. doi:10.1080/13668800802024652.

Guerci, M., A. B.(Rami) Shani, and L. Shani. 2014. "A Stakeholder Perspective for Sustainable HRM." In *Sustainability and Human Resource Management. Developing Sustainable Business Organizations*, edited by. I. Ehnert, W. Harry, and K. J. Zink 205–23. Berlin Heidelberg: Springer.

Guerci, M., and M. Pedrini. 2014. "The Consensus between Italian HR and Sustainability Managers on HR Management for Sustainability – Driven Change- towards a "Strong" HR Management System." *The International Journal of Human Resource Management* 25 (13):1787–814. doi:10.1080/09585192.2013.860388.

Guerci, M., G. Radaelli, E. Siletti, S. Cirella, and A. B.(Rami), Shani. 2015. "The Impact of Human Resource Management Practices and Corporate Sustainability on Organizational Ethical Climates: An Employee Perspective." *Journal of Business Ethics* 126 (2):325–42. doi:10.1007/s10551-013-1946-1.

Guest, D. 2002. "Human Resource Management, Corporate Performance and Employee Wellbeing: Building the Worker into HRM." *The Journal of Industrial Relations* 44 (3):335–58. doi:10.1111/1472-9296.00053.

Guest, D. E. 1997. "Human Resource Management and Performance: A Review and Research Agenda." *International Journal of Human Resource Management* 8 (3):263–76. doi:10.1080/095851997341630.

Guest, D. E. 2011. "Human Resource Management and Performance: Still Searching for Some Answers." *Human Resource Management Journal* 21 (1):3–13. doi:10.1111/j.1748-8583.2010.00164.x.

Guest, D. E. 2017. "Human Resource Management and Employee Well-Being: Towards a New Analytic Framework." *Human Resource Management Journal* 27 (1):22–38. doi:10.1111/1748-8583.12139.

Harry, W. 2014. "The Relevance of the Vision of Sustainability to HRM Practice." In *Sustainability and Human Resource Management. Developing Sustainable Business Organizations*, edited by I. Ehnert, W. Harry, and K.J. Zink 401–19. Berlin Heidelberg: Springer.

Jackson, S. E., and J. Seo. 2010. "The Greening of Strategic HRM Scholarship." *Organization Management Journal* 7 (4):278–90. doi:10.1057/omj.2010.37.

Jamal, M., and Baba, V. V. 1992. "Shiftwork and Department-Type Related to Job Stress, Work Attitudes and Behavioral Intentions: A Study of Nurses". *Journal of Organizational Behavior* 13 (5): 449–64.

Jamil, A., U. Raja, and W. Darr. 2013. "Psychological Contract Types as Moderator in the Breach-Violation and Violation-Burnout Relationships." *The Journal of Psychology* 147 (5):491–515. doi:10.1080/00223980.2012.717552.

Järlström, M., E. Saru, and S. Vanhala. 2018. "Sustainable Human Resource Management with Salience of Stakeholders: A Top Management Perspective." *Journal of Business Ethics* 152 (3):703–724. doi:10.1007/s10551-016-3310-8

Jensen, J. M., P. C. Patel, and J. G. Messersmith. 2013. "High-Performance Work Systems and Job Control: Consequences for Anxiety, Role Overload, and Turnover Intentions." *Journal of Management* 39 (6):1699–724. doi:10.1177/0149206311419663.

Jiang, K., D. P. Lepak, J. Hu, and J. C. Baer. 2012. "How Does Human Resource Management Influence Organizational Outcomes? A Meta-Analytic Investigation of Mediating Mechanisms." *Academy of Management Journal* 55 (6):1264–94. doi:10.5465/amj.2011.0088.

Kira, M., and S. Lifvergren. 2014. "Sowing seeds for sustainability in work systems." In *Sustainability and Human Resource Management. Developing Sustainable Business Organizations*, edited by I. Ehnert, W. Harry, and K. J. Zink, 57–81. Berlin Heidelberg: Springer.

Kopelman, R. E., Greenhaus, J. H., and Connolly, T. F. 1983. "A Model of Work, Family, and Interrole Conflict: A Construct Validation Study". *Organizational Behavior and Human Performance* 32 (2):198–215.

Kozica, A., and S. Kaiser. 2012. "A Sustainability Perspective in Flexible HRM: How to Cope with Paradoxes of Contingent Work." *Management Revu* 23 (3):239–61. doi:10.5771/0935-9915-2012-3-239.

Kramar, R. 2014. "Beyond Strategic Human Resource Management: Is Sustainable Human Resource Management the Next Approach?" *The International Journal of Human Resource Management* 25 (8):1069–89. doi:10.1080/09585192.2013.816863.

Kroon, B., K. Van de Voorde, and M. J. P. M. Van Veldhoven. 2009. "Cross-Level Effects of High-Performance Work Practices on Burnout: Two Counteracting Mediating Mechanisms Compared." *Personnel Review* 38 (5): 509–25. doi:10.1108/00483480910978027.

Legge, K. 1995. *Human Resource Management: Rhetorics and Realities.* Basingstoke: Macmillan

Macky, K., and P. Boxall. 2008. "High-Involvement Work Processes, Work Intensification and Employee Well-Being: A Study of New Zealand Worker Experiences." *Asia Pacific Journal of Human Resources* 46 (1):38–55. doi:10.1177/1038411107086542..

Mak, A., L. Cheung, A. Mak, and L. Leung. 2014. "Confucian Thinking and the Implications for Sustainability in HRM." *Asia-Pacific Journal of Business Administration* 6 (3):206–24.

Maley, J. 2014. "Sustainability: The Missing Element in Performance Management." *Asia-Pacific Journal of Business Administration* 6 (3):190–205. doi:10.1108/APJBA-03-2014-0040.

Mariappanadar, S. 2003. "Sustainable Human Resource Strategy: The Sustainable and Unsustainable Dilemmas." *International Journal of Social Economics* 30 (8):906–23. doi:10.1108/03068290310483779.

Mariappanadar, S. 2012a. "Harm of Efficiency Oriented HRM Practices on Stakeholders: An Ethical Issue for Sustainability." *Society and Business Review* 7 (2):168–84. doi:10.1108/17465681211237628.

Mariappanadar, S. 2012b. "The Harm Indicators of Negative Externality of Efficiency Focused Organizational Practices." *International Journal of Social Economics* 39 (3):209–20. doi:10.1108/03068291211199378.

Mariappanadar, S. 2014a. "The Model of Negative Externality for Sustainable HRM." In *Sustainability and Human Resource Management. Developing Sustainable Business Organizations,* edited by I. Ehnert, W. Harry, and K.J. Zink, 181–203. Berlin Heidelberg: Springer.

Mariappanadar, S. 2014b. "Stakeholder Harm Index: A Framework to Review Work Intensification from the Critical HRM Perspective." *Human Resource Management Review* 24 (4):313–29. doi:10.1016/j.hrmr.2014.03.009.

Mariappanadar, S., and R. Kramar. 2014. "Sustainable HRM: The Synthesis Effect of High Performance Work Systems on Organisational Performance and Employee Harm." *Asia-Pacific Journal of Business Administration* 6 (3):206–24. doi:10.1108/APJBA-03-2014-0039.

Maslach, C., W. B. Schaufeli, and M. P. Leiter. 2001. "Job Burnout." *Annual Review of Psychology* 52 (1):397–422.

Nink, M. 2015. "The German Workforce Has a Burnout Problem." *Business Journal.*

Olsen, K. M., and S.-A. Dahl. 2010. "Working Time: Implications for Sickness Absence and the Work–Family Balance." *International Journal of Social Welfare* 19 (1):45–53. doi:10.1111/j.1468-2397.2008.00619.x.

Ongori, H., and J. E. Agolla. 2008. "Occupational Stress in Organizations and Its Effects on Organizational Performance." *Journal of Management Research* 8 (3):123–35.

Paauwe, J. 2012. "HRM Als Leer- en Ontwikkelingstraject." *Tijdschrift Voor HRM* 15:11–2.

Pfeffer, J. 2010. "Building Sustainable Organizations: The Human Factor." *Academy of Management Perspectives* 24 (1):34–45. doi:10.5465/AMP.2010.50304415.

Rowan, J. R. 2000. "The Moral Foundation of Employee Rights." *Journal of Business Ethics* 24 (4):355–61. doi:10.1023/A:1006286315756.

Saks, A. M. 2006. "Antecedents and Consequences of Employee Engagement." *Journal of Managerial Psychology* 21 (7):600–19. doi:10.1108/02683940610690169.

Schaufeli, W. B., A. B. Bakker, and W. Van Rhenen. 2009. "How Changes in Job Demands and Resources Predict Burnout, Work Engagement, and Sickness Absenteeism." *Journal of Organizational Behavior* 30 (7):893–917. doi:10.1002/job.595.

Schaufeli, W. B., and A. B. Bakker. 2004. "Job Demands, Job Resources, and Their Relationship with Burnout and Engagement: A Multi-Sample Study." *Journal of Organizational Behavior* 25 (3):293–315. doi:10.1002/job.248.

Schaufeli, W. B., I. M. Martinez, A. M. Pinto, M. Salanova, and A. B. Bakker. 2002. "Burnout and Engagement in University Students. A Cross-National Study." *Journal of Cross-Cultural Psychology* 33 (5):464–81. doi:10.1177/0022022102033005003.

Schaufeli, W. B., M. P. Leiter, and C. Maslach. 2009. "Burnout: 35 Years of Research and Practice." *Career Development International* 14 (3):204–20. doi:10.1108/13620430910966406.

Suriyankietkaew, S., and G. C. Avery. 2014. "Leadership Practices Influencing Stakeholder Satisfaction in Thai SMEs." *Asia-Pacific Journal of Business Administration* 6 (3):247–61. doi:10.1108/APJBA-01-2014-0010.

Thom, N., and R. J. Zaugg. 2004. "Nachhaltiges und Innovatives Personalmanagement: Spitzengruppenbefragung in Europäischen Unternehmungen und Institutionen." In *Nachhaltiges Innovationsmanagement*, edited by E. J. Schwarz, 217–45. Wiesbaden: Gabler.

UNCED (United Nations Conference on environment and development). 1992. "The Rio Declaration on Environment and Development".

Van De Voorde, K., J. Paauwe, and M. Van Veldhoven. 2012. "Employee Well-Being and the HRM–Organizational Performance Relationship: A Review of Quantitative Studies." *International Journal of Management Reviews* 14 (4):391–407. doi:10.1111/j.1468-2370.2011.00322.x.

Wells, S. 2011. "HRM for Sustainability: Creating a New Paradigm." In *Readings in HRM and Sustainability*, edited by M. Clarke, 133–146. Prahran: Tilde University Press.

Zaugg, R. J. 2009. *Nachhaltiges Personalmanagement: Eine Neue Perspektive Und Empirische Exploration Des Human Resource Management*. Wiesbaden: Gabler.

Zaugg, R. J., A. Blum, and N. Thom. 2001. *Sustainability in Human Resource Management. Evaluation Report*. Berne: IOP-Press.

Zink, K. J. 2007. "From Total Quality Management to Corporate Sustainability Based on a Stakeholder Management." *Journal of Management History* 13 (4):394–401. doi:10.1108/17511340710819615.

Zink, K. J. 2014. "Designing Sustainable Work Systems: The Need for a Systems Approach." *Applied Ergonomics* 45 (1):126–32.

Mental Construal and Employee Engagement: For More Engagement Look at the Big Picture

Shiva Taghavi

Abstract: This article links research in cognitive and social psychology to that in human resources management by proposing a conceptual model of the impact of mental construal on employee engagement. Based on construal-level theory, I suggest that an abstract mindset can facilitate the process of employee engagement in task work. Specifically, I address the effect of abstract representation of the work situation in an individual's mind on the features of engagement as being cognitive (attention, self-regulation, commitment, and job involvement), affective (positive affectivity), and behavioral (organizational citizenship behavior, role extension, and prosocial behavior). I also briefly discuss the importance of task characteristics. The proposed model offers new possibilities for human resources practices by introducing relatively new psychological techniques that can impact employees' attitudes and behaviors in the workplace.

INTRODUCTION

The concept of employee engagement has attracted the interest of many scholars and practitioners in recent years. Engagement has been shown to correlate highly with employee performance and psychological state, as well as with organizational outcomes such as turnover and financial performance (e.g., Harter, Schmidt, and Hayes 2002; Saks 2006). Recently, extensive work has explored the antecedents and consequences of engagement (Dalal et al. 2008; Macey and Schneider 2008; Saks 2006).

Using a self-regulatory perspective, Dalal et al. (2008) proposed that engagement is strongly associated with the attention paid to the task. Considered as a psychological state, engagement affects attention during the active self-regulation period but diminishes over time, and thus needs to be reactivated. "Research on state engagement should therefore focus on the factors that temporarily deplete or replenish a person's ability to regulate his or her attention toward the task" (Dalal et al. 2008, 53). The aim of this conceptual research is to elaborate on cognitive strategies that can affect attention and engagement. I show how methods that have been discussed in social and cognitive psychology, such as priming values and activating mindsets, could be employed in work settings to influence the state engagement.

First, drawing on construal level theory (Trope and Liberman 2003), I propose that activating an abstract mindset would be beneficial for the cognitive features of engagement (self-regulation, task commitment, and job involvement). Second, I explain the impact of this psychological process on the antecedents and consequences of engagement, as developed by Macey and Schneider (2008), namely positive affectivity, organizational citizenship behavior, role expansion, and prosocial behavior. Third, relying on research on priming (e.g.,. Bargh and Chartrand 2000), I discuss the methods by which priming values could impact engagement, and how an abstract mindset reinforces this value activation. Fourth, I discuss the importance of contextual factors, namely task characteristics.

MENTAL CONSTRUAL AND EMPLOYEE ENGAGEMENT

Construal Level Theory

According to construal level theory (Trope and Liberman 2003), events and objects can be represented at different levels in an individual's mind. More distal concepts, remote from direct experience, are understood on a higher level and involve more construal. This happens because, normally, we have less knowledge about the distant future and past, faraway places and people, and less imaginable alternatives to reality. This lack of knowledge about more remote events, places, and alternatives results in a more abstract representation of them. More proximal entities, however, involve less construal and are represented in a more concrete way due to the more detailed knowledge available and the feasibility of experimentation. This distance is, of course, beyond our physical understanding of space and time. It is, in fact, a subjective measure, depending on psychological, cognitive, and motivational factors. Studies on construal level and distance indicate that psychological distance correlates positively with level of construal. Distal entities are construed on a higher level than proximal entities (Liberman, Trope, and Stephan 2007). In this sense, psychological distance refers to subjective perceptions of an entity's temporal, spatial, social, and/or hypothetical proximity.

High level construal results in an abstract conceptualization of information about events and objects. Low level construal, in contrast, leads to concrete conceptualizations. Because abstract representations capture and highlight the superordinate central features of objects and events, high-level construal is more concerned about general meanings. These representations tend to be simpler, less ambiguous, more coherent and more schematic because irrelevant, inconsistent details have been omitted. Low-level construal, however, concentrates on processes, procedures, and exemplars, by highlighting the subordinate peripheral characteristics of the event or object. Thus, while a concrete mindset looks for how, the abstract mindset seeks why. In this regard, psychological distance is one of the core elements of the theory. Activation of high- or low-level construal depends on how and to what extent the event is perceived as far or close (in time, space, social distance, or even hypothetical aspect). The further the event, the more likely the perceiver is to construe the situation on a high, abstract level (Fujita et al. 2006; Levin-Sagi 2006; Trope and Liberman 2003, 2010).

Level of Mental Construal and Cognitive Engagement

Engagement has been shown to affect individuals' cognition in many ways (Dalal et al. 2008; Macey and Schneider 2008). Research on employee engagement conceptualizes employee engagement as being highly associated with organizational commitment, organizational identification, job involvement, and empowerment. Dalal et al. (2008) suggest that engagement corresponds to attention, and hence has a self-regulatory aspect. In this sense, in order to be engaged, the employee needs to focus intensely on the task and withdraw attention to do otherwise.

At the same time, research on construal level demonstrates that there is a positive and significant relationship between high-level construal mindset and self-control (Fujita et al. 2006; Haws 2007; Levin-Sagi 2006; Schmeichel, Vohs, and Duke 2011). In this sense, when two opposing motivations are in conflict, two levels of mental construal are, in fact, in opposition. For example, the need to work hard to meet a deadline could be opposed to the tendency to take a break every 10 min. Accordingly, the self-control conflict occurs between high- and low-level construal, or in other words, it is a conflict between "valance attached to primary, central, goal-relevant, superordinate considerations" (high-level construal) and "valance attached to secondary, incidental, goal-irrelevant, subordinated features" (low-level construal) (Trope and Liberman 2010). Thus, if preparing the report is related to superordinate goals and taking coffee breaks is a secondary, goal-irrelevant motivation, then the latter behavior would be a failure of self-control. A series of studies by Fujita et al. demonstrate that activating higher-level construal increases self-control (Fujita et al. 2006). Consequently, an employee who is at a higher construal level gives more weight to primary and central goals, or performance, than secondary, peripheral ones.

> **Proposition 1.** An abstract mindset positively affects employee engagement through increasing attentional pull and self-regulation.

Engagement is highly associated with organizational commitment and job involvement. In this sense, scholars conceptualize commitment as the willingness to exert energy as well as the feeling of pride and a high level of identification with the organization (Macey and Schneider 2008). An abstract mindset leads individuals to perceive actions with regard to their superordinate meanings and goals. It also helps them generate positive ideas in favor of the action.

Studies show that arguing in favor of or against an action is associated with construal level. In a series of experiments, Eyal and his colleagues show that considerations in favor of an action (pros) are superordinate to considerations against the action (Eyal et al. 2004; Routledge et al. 2010). These studies demonstrate that people in an abstract mindset tend to generate more advantages than drawbacks for a given action. In another study Herzog,

Hansen, and Wange (2007) show that when the action is being perceived in the more distant future (higher construal level) it is easier to generate ideas in favor of the action, and more difficult to generate ideas against it.

As a result, employees who perceive their responsibilities at a higher level of mental construal consider them from a more holistic perspective and take into account the value and importance of the outcomes for their career and the organization. Therefore, since they construe their work at a higher level and perceive it to be central to their self, employees with an abstract mindset are more motivated to get involved with the task and perform more productively with respect to higher-order goals. Thus, I put forth the following proposition:

Proposition 2. A higher mental construal level results in greater commitment and job involvement, and consequently greater employee engagement.

Mental Construal Level and Affective Antecedent of Engagement

Engagement, both as a dispositional trait and a psychological state, has a strong affective dimension. Positive affectivity, which connotes components of activation and pleasantness (Larsen and Diener 1992), is the main affective element of the state engagement, as well as its dispositional antecedent (Macey and Schneider 2008).

Construal level theory suggests that emotions can arise from low or high construal level. In this sense, emotions such as love and pride require abstract, high-level construal of the emotion-eliciting situation. Moreover, higher level emotions decay less sharply over time (Trope and Liberman 2010).

Based on Macey and Schneider's (2008) conceptualization of the state engagement, its affective element indicates that it involves feelings of persistence, vigor, energy, dedication, absorption, enthusiasm, alertness, and pride.

Therefore, when a situation is represented at a higher level of mental construal, the individual would automatically value higher level affects, such as pride, dedication, and enthusiasm. In this sense, we expect individuals at a higher level of mental construal to experience more positive affectivity. Therefore, I propose the following proposition:

Proposition 3. An abstract mindset increases positive affectivity—indicating feelings of persistence, vigor, energy, dedication, absorption, enthusiasm, alertness, and pride—and therefore increases employee engagement.

Mental Construal Level and Behavioral Consequences of Engagement

Organizational Citizenship Behavior (OCB) and prosocial and extra-role behaviors are the major facets of employee engagement (Macey and Schneider 2008). Although Macey and Schneider termed such behaviors as "behavioral engagement," Dalal et al. (2008) argued that they are in fact "behavioral consequences" of engagement, since engagement "is a cognitive-affective construct, not a . . . behavioral one" (55) Regardless of how we label them, these behaviors all connote the notion of "going above and beyond" the enforceable requirements of the job description and what is normally expected.

Construal level theory would suggest that when people identify things on a higher level of mental construal, they conceptualize them in an abstract, holistic way. I suggest that this global mindset facilitates the process of "going the extra mile," and therefore broadens the individual's attention to a wider range of non-routine, untypical tasks.

> **Proposition 4.** Individuals at a higher level of mental construal exhibit more positive organizational citizenship behavior, role-extension, and prosocial behavior.

Priming Values, Abstract Mindsets, and State Engagement

Research on implicit cognition demonstrates that goals, motives, stereotypes, and traits can be implicitly and unconsciously activated in the presence of situational cues and can eventually drive behavior (Bargh and Chartrand 1999; Bargh, Chen, and Burrows 1996; Chartrand and Bargh 1996).

Studies show that when activated, values can invoke behaviors (Verplanken and Holland 2002), though the effect found was not very strong and was moderated by variables such as self-centrality, interactions between social values, and reasons supporting the importance of the values (Darley and Batson 1973; Maio et al. 2001).

More relevant to this research, the abstract mindset boosts the effect of activated value on behavior (Torelli and Kaikati 2009). Torelli and Kaikati (2009) activated values and abstract mindset simultaneously, and observed an increase in value-congruent judgments and behaviors. Though they induced abstract and concrete mindsets using a different manipulation from that used for value activation, I would argue that, in general, values are superordinate goals. Hence, they will automatically trigger an abstract mindset. An abstract mindset, in turn, improves the effect of activated values on behavior. Higher construal level not only boosts the consistency between triggered values and behavior, but also directly affects cognition, and consequently behavior. When an action is represented at a higher level of mental construal, people will automatically give more weight to long-term goals and the desirability of the action, and it will be easier for them to generate thoughts and arguments in favor of the action. In this sense, we expect that when values involving hard work (e.g., religious or cultural values) are activated, individuals perceive the work at a higher level of mental construal, and consequently experience a more positive work attitude, and engagement.

Task Characteristics, Mindset, and State Engagement

So far, I have discussed the importance of abstract mindset with regard to employee engagement. Although this article proposes that an abstract mindset influences cognitive, affective, and behavioral engagement positively, the characteristics of the task could moderate this effect.

Research on goal-setting and motivational techniques indicates that the relationship between task difficulty and task performance is one of the main drivers of motivation. This relationship seems to be rather complicated, being moderated and mediated by many factors.

Initially, Atkinson (1958) showed that task difficulty, measured as the probability of success in the task, has an inverse U-shaped relationship with task performance. However, (Locke and Latham 1990; Locke 2002) found that task complexity moderates the link between the goal and the performance, in the sense that, the effect of higher level goals on task performance is greater for simple than for complex tasks. One factor that can facilitate performance in the case of complex tasks is to set a proximal goal rather than "do-your-best," or distal goals. Latham and Seijts (1999) used a business game as a moderately complex task to show that performance is significantly higher when the goal is proximal (when there are more detailed goals for each stage of the task) than when the goal is distal (when the goals indicate the task's overall objectives).

Another research stream, action identification theory (Vallacher and Wegner 2014), identifies simple tasks at a higher, more abstract level. Action Identification theory, which is one of the foundations of construal level theory, suggests that actions can be identified at different levels based on their cognitive representation in the agent's mind. That is, lower action identity levels cover the specific details of the action, whereas higher identity levels imply a more general, abstract perception of the action. The theory suggests that individuals are able to perform the act in accordance with their own values only if they identify the higher, broader meanings of the action.

A correlational study has shown that the action's identity level significantly correlates with the perceived characteristics of the action: difficulty, familiarity, complexity, duration, and learning time. Thus, the more the action is perceived as difficult, new, and complex, the lower the level chosen to maintain the action (Wegner and Vallacher 1986). As a result of practice, or inherent simplicity of the action, individuals will maintain easy actions at a higher level of identification, because the details of how to perform the action are automatic. Hence, easy, familiar and more frequent tasks will be performed more efficiently by people who identify them at a higher, more abstract level.

Moreover, higher action identification level, or in the terminology of construal level theory, higher construal level, concerns task desirability, whereas low action identification level, or low construal level, concerns task feasibility (Liberman and Trope 1998). Abstract construal leads to increased enjoyment of the task, whereas concrete construal involves the details and resources that make the task more feasible. Therefore, when the task is easy, familiar and repetitive, an abstract mindset is more beneficial, because it is more consistent with the way people need to identify this type of action.

Thus, while it has been argued that activating an abstract mindset is more beneficial for employee engagement, it is also important to consider task characteristics. Future research should explore the level of abstractness that needs to be activated for optimal engagement, without negatively impacting the performance of specific tasks.

Contribution, Limitations, and Future Directions

This article aimed to link two streams of research in organizational psychology, namely cognitive and social psychological oriented research on mindset, and organizational research on employee engagement. Based on the literature in organizational and job engagement, this work suggests that an abstract mindset boosts cognitive, affective and behavioral engagement. In particular, I propose that an abstract mindset increases the attention paid to task work, enhances job commitment and involvement, boosts positive affectivity and mood, and finally affects organizational citizenship, and prosocial and extra-role behavior.

This article contributes to the literature on employee engagement by highlighting one possible technique for increasing job engagement, that of activating an abstract mindset. Although this article does not address the practical aspects of implementing this psychological technique, it discusses in detail the link between construal level and psychological distance, which can be temporal, spatial, social, and/or hypothetical. The more distant people perceive actions to be, the higher the mental construal level (Trope and Liberman 2010). In the organizational context, perceptions of distance can be activated temporally (e.g., raises and promotion, which are expected in future) as well as socially (e.g., identification with the organization, to trigger a sense of social distance from outgroups). On the other hand, values and ideologies can also activate an abstract mindset. Because of their abstract, decontextualized nature, values are more likely to channel mental representation to a higher level (Eyal et al. 2009).

Further studies are required to investigate practical methods of mindset priming within organizations. Therefore, future research should focus on the impact of mental construal on organizational and job engagement by conducting field studies to take account of environmental factors. One of the main limitations of this research is that it only focuses on job engagement. Future research could investigate the impact of construal level on organizational engagement.

ACKNOWLEDGMENTS

The author thanks EIASM for organizing the Workshop for Strategic Human Resource Management that provided the opportunity to engage in this discussion. I also thank the French Investissements d'Avenir (ANR-11-IDEX-0003/Labex Ecodec/ANR-11-LABX-0047) for funding our working meetings to produce this article. Additionally, I thank HEC Paris School of Management and NEOMA Business School for their support of this research.

REFERENCES

Atkinson, J. W. 1958. "Towards experimental analysis of human motivation in terms of motives, expectancies, and incentives." In *Motives in Fantasy, action and Society.*, edited by J.W. Atkinson, 288–305. Princeton, NJ: Van Nostrand.

Bargh, J. A., and T. L. Chartrand. 1999. "The Unbearable Automaticity of Being." *American Psychologist* 54 (7): 462. doi: 10.1037/0003-066X.54.7.462.

Bargh, J. A., and T. L. Chartrand. 2000. "Studying the Mind in the Middle: A Practical Guide to Priming and Automaticity Research." *Handbook of Research Methods in Social Psychology* :253–85.

Bargh, J. A., M. Chen, and L. Burrows. 1996. "Automaticity of Social Behavior: Direct Effects of Trait Construct and Stereotype Activation on Action." *Journal of Personality and Social Psychology* 71 (2):230. doi: 10.1037/0022-3514.71.2.230.

Chartrand, T. L., and J. A. Bargh. 1996. "Automatic Activation of Impression Formation and Memorization Goals: Nonconscious Goal Priming Reproduces Effects of Explicit Task Instructions." *Journal of Personality and Social Psychology* 71 (3):464. doi: 10.1037/0022-3514.71.3.464.

Dalal, R. S., B. J. Brummel, S. Wee, and L. L. Thomas. 2008. "Defining Employee Engagement for Productive Research and Practice." *Industrial and Organizational Psychology* 1 (01):52–5. doi: 10.1111/j.1754-9434.2007.00008.x.

Darley, John M., and C. Daniel Batson. 1973. "From Jerusalem to Jericho": a Study of Situational and Dispositional Variables in Helping Behavior." *Journal of Personality and Social Psychology* 27 (1):100–8. doi: 10.1037/h0034449.

Eyal, T., N. Liberman, Y. Trope, and E. Walther. 2004. "The Pros and Cons of Temporally near and Distant Action." *Journal of Personality and Social Psychology* 86 (6):781.

Eyal, T., M. D. Sagristano, Y. Trope, N. Liberman, and S. Chaiken. 2009. "When Values Matter: Expressing Values in Behavioral Intentions for the near vs. distant Future." *Journal of Experimental Social Psychology* 45 (1):35–43. doi: 10.1016/j.jesp.2008.07.023.

Fujita, K., Y. Trope, N. Liberman, and M. Levin-Sagi. 2006. "Construal Levels and self-control." *Journal of Personality and Social Psychology* 90 (3):351.

Harter, J. K., F. L. Schmidt, and T. L. Hayes. 2002. "Business-unit-level Relationship between Employee Satisfaction, employee Engagement, and Business Outcomes: A Meta-Analysis." *Journal of Applied Psychology* 87 (2):268. doi: 10.1037/0021-9010.87.2.268.

Haws, K. 2007. "A Construal Level Theory Approach to Understanding Self-Control Strategies." *Advances in Consumer Research* 34:334.

Herzog, S. M., J. Hansen, and M. Wanke. 2007. "Temporal Distance and Ease of Retrieval." *Journal of Experimental Social Psychology* 43 (3):483–8. doi: 10.1016/j.jesp.2006.05.008.

Larsen, R. J., and E. Diener. 1992. "Promises and problems with the circumplex model of emotion."

Latham, G. P., and G. H. Seijts. 1999. "The Effects of Proximal and Distal Goals on Performance on a Moderately Complex Task." *Journal of Organizational Behavior* 20 (4):421–9. doi: 10.1002/(SICI)1099-1379(199907)20:4<421::AID-JOB896>3.0.CO;2-#.

Levin-Sagi, M. 2006. "*Construal Level Theory and a Comprehensive Approach to Self-Control.*" Tel Aviv University.

Liberman, N., and Y. Trope. 1998. "The role of feasibility and desirability considerations in near and distant future decisions: A test of temporal construal theory." *Journal of Personality and Social Psychology* 75 (1):5.

Liberman, N., Y. Trope, and E. Stephan. 2007. "Psychological distance."

Locke, K. 2002. "The grounded theory approach to qualitative research." *Measuring and Analyzing Behavior in Organizations., Jossey-Bass, San Francisco, CA*:17–43.

Locke, E. A., and G. P. Latham. 1990. *A Theory of Goal Setting & task Performance:*. Prentice-Hall, Inc.

Macey, W. H., and B. Schneider. 2008. "The Meaning of Employee Engagement." *Industrial and Organizational Psychology* 1 (01):3–30. doi: 10.1111/j.1754-9434.2007.0002.x.

Maio, G. R., J. M. Olson, L. Allen, and M. M. Bernard. 2001. "Addressing Discrepancies between Values and Behavior: The Motivating Effect of Reasons* 1,* 2." *Journal of Experimental Social Psychology* 37 (2):104–17. doi: 10.1006/jesp.2000.1436.

Routledge, Clay, Brian Ostafin, Jacob Juhl, Constantine Sedikides, Christie Cathey, and Jiangqun Liao. 2010. "Adjusting to Death: The Effects of Mortality Salience and Self-Esteem on Psychological Well-Being, Growth Motivation, and Maladaptive Behavior." *Journal of Personality and Social Psychology* 99 (6):897–916. doi: 10.1037/a0021431.

Saks, A. M. 2006. "Antecedents and Consequences of Employee Engagement." *Journal of Managerial Psychology* 21 (7):600–19. doi: 10.1108/02683940610690169.

Schmeichel, B. J., K. D. Vohs, and S. C. Duke. 2011. "Self-Control at High and Low Levels of Mental Construal." *Social Psychological and Personality Science* 2 (2):182. doi: 10.1177/1948550610385955.

Torelli, Carlos J., and Andrew M. Kaikati. 2009. "Values as Predictors of Judgments and Behaviors: The Role of Abstract and Concrete Mindsets." *Journal of Personality and Social Psychology* 96 (1):231–47. doi: 10.1037/a0013836.

Trope, Y., and N. Liberman. 2003. "Temporal construal." *Psychological Review* 110 (3):403.

Trope, Y., and N. Liberman. 2010. "Construal-level Theory of Psychological Distance." *Psychological Review* 117 (2):440. doi: 10.1037/a0018963.

Vallacher, R. R., and D. M. Wegner. 2014. *A Theory of Action Identification.* Psychology Press. Erlbaum.

Verplanken, B., and R. W. Holland. 2002. "Motivated Decision Making: Effects of Activation and Self-centrality of Values on Choices and Behavior." *Journal of Personality and Social Psychology* 82 (3):434. doi: 10.1037/0022-3514.82.3.434.

Wegner, D. M., and R. R. Vallacher. 1986. "Action Identification." In *Handbook of Motivation and Cognition: Foundations of Social Behavior*, edited by R. M. Sorrentino and E. T. Higgins, 550–82. New York, NY US: Guilford Press.

The Future of Employee Engagement: Real-Time Monitoring and Digital Tools for Engaging a Workforce

Jennifer R. Burnett and Timothy C. Lisk

Abstract: At no other time have organizations had so much opportunity to measure and evaluate the effectiveness and efficiency of their workforce. While not all companies have yet to embrace the tools and technology available to them, leading companies have been able to capitalize on new technologies that track productivity, sales, customer satisfaction, work flows, quality, and workplace interactions on a frequent, sometimes real time basis. Additionally, the tools to synthesize and analyze this data has also rapidly advanced in the last few years with the more mainstream availability of statistical modeling, machine learning technology, and artificial intelligence applications. Yet, when it comes to measuring and tracking employee engagement, most companies still evaluate engagement on an annual, or longer, basis using traditional survey techniques. While these practices have provided a wealth of insight into the dimensions and impact of engagement, it is time to rethink how we are measuring engagement and, more importantly, how the same digital tools can be applied towards improving the productivity, retention, and satisfaction of the workforce. We propose a series of research topics to address this modern trend of the impact of technological advances on both the measurement of engagement and the application of human resource management (HRM) practices to improve engagement.

EMPLOYMENT ENGAGEMENT: HOW FAR HAVE WE COME?

At no other time have organizations had so much opportunity to measure and evaluate the effectiveness and efficiency of their workforce. While not all companies have yet to embrace the tools and technology available to them, leading companies have been able to capitalize on new technologies that track productivity, sales, customer satisfaction, work flows, quality, and workplace interactions on a frequent, sometimes real-time basis. Key strokes on computers, transactions with customers, production time, and more are measured using advanced and wearable technology. The tools to synthesize and analyze this data has also rapidly advanced in the last few years with the more mainstream availability of statistical modeling, machine learning technology, and artificial intelligence applications. Yet, when it comes to measuring and tracking employee engagement, most companies have not advanced and still evaluate engagement on an annual, or longer, basis, using traditional survey techniques. While these practices have provided a wealth of insight into the dimensions and impact of engagement, it is time to rethink how we are measuring engagement and, more importantly, applying the results towards improving the productivity, retention, and satisfaction of the workforce.

The idea that people who are satisfied and happy with their jobs and careers are also more likely to be productive and stay with an organization most likely dates back to before we created a way to measure this concept. It seems very rational that individuals who are not happy with their job or company, would not work as hard, or not be as motivated to provide exceptional service to customers, or to ensure that the work was done to the best of their abilities. As human beings, we will move towards and stay with those activities that bring us satisfaction and fulfillment, and move away from those that do not. However, employment is a little bit different than the other choices we make in our lives. Most people need to be employed or have some source of income to meet their basic needs in life, and are willing to tolerate a little dissatisfaction for a decent paycheck. From an employers' viewpoint, however, we know that these dissatisfied, disengaged employees can cause more harm than good, and at some point we decided that we needed to know the level of satisfaction and commitment of our employee population so that action could be taken to minimize those risks, or reverse the trend.

Employee engagement today is still defined in many ways. We have yet to identify a standard definition. Some definitions focus on the internal, emotional state of the employee and include employees' feelings such as the following ones:

- enthusiasm
- commitment
- dedication
- motivation
- passion
- satisfaction
- fulfillment

Other definitions link the employees' emotional state to outcomes such as the following ones:

- long term tenure
- productivity
- positive action to further the organizations' reputation and interest
- positive customer interactions
- discretionary effort into their work
- efforts that contribute to organizational success

- efforts that contribute to individual and organizational performance, productivity and well-being
- working on behalf of the organizations' goals

(Albrecht 2010; Christian, Garza, and Slaughter, 2011, Macey et al. 2009)

Engagement also has been shown to be highly related to various constructs such as the following ones:

- job satisfaction
- organizational commitment
- organizational citizenship
- employee morale
- employee motivation

Furthermore, the concept of engagement has been differentiated at the individual, team and organizational level, due to the desire to influence and improve engagement for both a person and in aggregate (Bakker, Van Emmerick, and Euewema, 2006). If engagement, regardless of having a standard definition, was going to be something that organizational leaders could influence, then identifying potential predictors and drivers of engagement became as important as measuring engagement itself. In a 2006 Conference Board Report, 12 studies that were conducted between 2003 and 2005 were cited in their analysis. Across those 12 studies, 26 different drivers of engagement were included. The analysis indicated that 8 key factors were identified in at least 4 of the studies as significantly impacting engagement. They included: trust and integrity, relationship with one's manager, influence of coworkers/team members, pride about the company, employee development, career growth opportunities, nature of the job, and alignment between individual and company performance. The more emotional drivers tended to have a greater impact on discretionary effort than did rational drivers.

Today we can see how this and other research has resulted in the development of various versions of engagement surveys which quickly gained popularity in the United States and worldwide, by organizations such as Gallup, Kenexa, Aon Hewitt, and Towers Perrin. These survey tools address the multifaceted aspects of engagement, not only of the individual's engagement to their work, but also to the organization, and addresses potential drivers and antecedents as well. The Utrecht Work Engagement Scale (UWES) also became more widely used for academic purposes, but primarily measures the construct of work engagement of vigor, dedication, and absorption (Schaufeli, Bakker, and Salanova 2006).

Once there were more widely acceptable tools and practices available to corporations, and buy-in from human resource and talent leaders that these concepts were important for guiding talent practices, and outcomes, it was critical to make the business case that engagement of employees could indeed impact the success of the business.

WHY SHOULD ORGANIZATIONAL LEADERS CARE ABOUT EMPLOYEE ENGAGEMENT?

The idea that engaged employees lead to happy customers and/or better business results seems somewhat intuitive. There also is a great deal of evidence that demonstrates those relationships are indeed true (Albrecht et al. 2015).

At the individual level, a person's satisfaction and engagement with their job and employer plays a significant role in their decision to show up for work, to put forth their most productive effort, to stay with the organization, and to positively influence the work environment and culture. Highly engaged employees tend to outperform their disengaged coworkers by 20–30% (Silvis 2016). Conversely, a recent study by Cornerstone Inc. indicated that a toxic employee has not only a negative impact on the team performance but also can result in good employees leaving the organization to escape having to work with that individual (Cornerstone OnDemand, 2016).

Large scale shifts and improvements of engagement are more likely to impact broader business level outcomes such as financial results, revenue, customer satisfaction, and competitiveness in the market. The collective engagement of an organization's employees is often intricately tied to their culture, their brand, and their employer value proposition–all of which reflect outwardly in the market and shape their reputation and image.

At this organizational level, the research is even more compelling. Macey et al. (2009) presented evidence of the impact of an engaged workforce on return on assets ROA and other financial metrics. Gallup's latest meta-analysis shows important differences in productivity, safety, customer satisfaction, and profitability when business units with high employee engagement are compared to business units with low engagement (Harter et al. 2016). In that regard, engagement has become very important, even to C-suite leaders, as one of few levers they feel they can influence to not only address their talent needs around retaining and growing a productive workforce, but they also recognize the impact on business outcomes.

BUT DO ALL THESE EFFORTS REALLY WORK?

According to Deloitte's recent report, 79% of companies included in their report measure engagement annually or less frequently, and 14% are not measuring engagement at all (Deloitte 2017). Typically, when a large organization begins to measure employee engagement, the process itself of collecting the survey responses, analyzing and reviewing the results, and then creating actionable steps for change and improvement, takes a year or more. This time frame may be shorter for smaller or more nimble organizations. However, especially if it is the first-time engagement is being measured, there is a lot of information to be taken into consideration, as mentioned previously.

Actions may result in large-scale human capital investments, such as implementing new practices around learning and development and career-pathing, or more specific behavioral changes like demonstrating real-time appreciation and recognition for a job well done. The results impact all areas of the company and expectations for change often fall upon frontline managers and leaders.

Engagement results may also shed light on significant cultural issues which are more challenging to address and overcome. Identifying beliefs and values that may be harming your business results, reputation, brand, customer retention, or investor confidence can be met with resistance or disbelief from leaders. Companies may struggle with interpreting exactly what the survey results mean for them and while recommendations and best practices for change are readily available, they may still be anecdotal rather than grounded in actual results.

On the opposite end of the spectrum, some organizations are asking if a workforce could be too engaged. The too-much-of-a-good-thing (TMGT; Pierce and Aguinis 2013) effect notes that many organizational relationships appear to have a curvilinear relationship rather than the simplistic linear relationship often touted in management circles. Engagement interventions, therefore, may at best offer diminishing returns and at worst blithely pursue a counter-productive course of action. However, TGMT does not seem to be a concern among most organizations for now. At the organizational level, we clearly have not solved the employee engagement equation (Aon Hewitt 2017). But that does not mean we should ignore the issue—while global engagement may be down, that does not preclude the possibility that pockets of overengaged employees may exist within organizations or that the cultures of some firms may reinforce TMGT when it comes to satisfaction, engagement, and commitment.

Regardless of the results, any change effort designed to improve engagement is likely to require time and resources. Initially, especially in the first few years of measuring engagement, corporate leaders tend to understand that the impact on business outcomes will not be realized immediately. Engagement is a lagging, not leading indicator, and therefore, the drivers of engagement will need to change, then engagement, and then outcomes such as productivity, quality, and customer satisfaction. The process requires patience.

However, some practitioners are beginning to question this long cycle of measure, analysis and action. Their ability to also measure the impact of the action may cause frustration. In fact, when engagement trends are tracked over time, there is not typically a large change at the organizational level. According to the Gallup Daily Tracking Tool, which polls by phone 1,500 employed adults per day (http://www.gallup.com/poll/180404/gallup-daily-employee-engagement.aspx), there is not much variation in engagement in the last year, or two years, for that matter. It seems to fluctuate between 30% and 35% engaged workers, with a bit of a peak at the beginning of 2017.

Furthermore, when engagement and/or its drivers are measured infrequently, other mediating or moderating factors may not be as evident. Shifts in corporate strategy, such as acquiring other companies or being acquired, have been shown to impact engagement (Aon Hewitt 2013). An influx of new employees also can have an impact on team and organizational engagement (Albrecht et al. 2015). Being able to measure, analyze, track, and act upon those meaningful fluctuations is necessary for an organization to make more timely changes to their practices and processes that are impacting the overall worker experience.

Finally, if we accept that our comprehensive measures of engagement are lagging indicators, then what should we be measuring and holding managers accountable for impacting? The answer to this question will most likely vary by organization and will be dependent on those engagement drivers previously identified. The key is to identify those factors that you are directly trying to impact in the short term, and that are within the control and influence of the organizational people leaders.

TECHNOLOGICAL ADVANCEMENTS ENHANCE THE MEASUREMENTS AND ANALYSIS OF EMPLOYEE ENGAGEMENT

One of the top priorities of corporate leaders today is to create and design their organizations to keep up with the rapid pace of change in technology and in the global marketplace. Ensuring that their workforce is prepared for those new challenges is top of mind for executives, according to Deloitte's 2017 Global Human Capital Trends Report. This new organization requires a high level of agility and collaboration by the workforce. Work will be designed based on more natural types of networks and interaction to maximize productivity, innovation, and change. The impact on the larger ecosystem is significant as the new organization of the future depends on changes to organizational design, work design, talent mobility, and the use of advanced technologies that will enable the new organization. For the organizations themselves, the challenge is that this new way of doing business takes time, is highly dynamic, will be met with resistance, and, in many cases, may fail. Failure will be clearly evident, however, in that those organizations who cannot adapt will no longer be able to compete, or perhaps even survive.

Organizations with highly engaged workforces have an advantage in this new ecosystem, in that there is also evidence that they are more adaptable than their counterparts (Macey et al. 2009). Additionally, highly motivated, committed employees are more likely to engage in continuous learning and development activities, particularly when they see the long-term benefit to the organization as well as their own careers. These behaviors are critical for the workforce of the future to succeed. This new pressure, coupled with criticism that engagement may be more difficult to change than originally believed, creates a new opportunity to rethink the way we measure, analyze, and influence employee engagement, at the individual, team, and organizational levels.

Practical implications are already evident, as organizations want to keep a true pulse on fluctuations of their employee populations' level of engagement, and address any shifts in real time. This practical desire, driven by the speed of business, and the technical capabilities available today, has resulted in an increase in the practice to measure engagement using more targeted, on-demand methods. We suggest that the maximum impact of interventions to improve engagement, and, as a result, important business outcomes, occurs when the following conditions are fulfilled:

• Engagement, satisfaction, and commitment are measured frequently through a multi-method approach;

- Engagement, satisfaction, and commitment results are integrated with HR analytics to provide robust models of drivers of engagement;
- Managers are held accountable for improvements in key talent management metrics, rather than improvements in engagement, commitment, or satisfaction.

Embracing these practices, as many organizations already are today, allows corporate leaders to create more targeted and timely interventions for improving engagement, satisfaction, commitment, and ultimately productivity, retention, customer satisfaction, and financial results.

PRACTICAL QUESTIONS NEEDING RIGOROUS RESEARCH

While annual surveys may effectively capture employees' enduring engagement, they may not be enough. Engagement can be impacted by multiple factors in the workplace and fluctuating individual factors as well (Bakker and Bal 2010). Therefore, timing of the measurement of engagement is an important consideration for the accuracy of interpretation of results. Additionally, as noted previously, engagement measures today are primarily lagging, rather than leading, indicators and could provide more insight if measured more frequently. Sonnentag (2003) was one of the first researchers to indicate the variation in engagement of employees on a daily basis. Bakker (2014) used diary research to show how fluctuations in engagement are a function of daily changes in job and personal resources, and described this as daily shifting of the "state of vigor, dedication, and absorption." As a result, the frequent measurement of engagement and the drivers of engagement have started to become more acceptable, particularly with the advancement of technologies that support this type of frequent measurement, called "pulse" surveys. Pulse surveys are still surveys but only gather information on very succinct topics or constructs. The idea is to elicit more real time responses from representative samples of the employee population to at least allow a more frequent tracking of the state of engagement. This approach is often used to specifically measure the impact of an intervention or change. For example, if an annual survey indicates that employees express a higher likelihood to leave the organization and that is linked to the lack of clarity regarding future career opportunities, then the company may create and implement a new program related to career development and advancement. Post implementation, finding out if there is a positive change in the way in which employees perceive their career opportunities may be used as a short-term way to determine the success of the initiative. Pulse surveys may also be used to track the same dimensions as the annual survey, but instead the intention is to determine fluctuations or perhaps factors that may influence those sentiments on a more real time basis. As a result, the organization can intervene in a more timely way. Research is needed to determine whether this more frequent, targeted measurement of individual and team level engagement does in fact result in organizations being able to more accurately identify short term drivers of engagement, as well as satisfaction and commitment, and take action to impact the improvement of engagement.

Connecting feedback to action can be challenging in an environment where frequent, pulse feedback is the norm. When ones' employer is continually collecting feedback, it can become difficult to connect the actions of the organization to any one piece of feedback. To address this, some organizations are beginning to shift their focus from three to five key drivers, addressed via organizational interventions on an annual or biannual cadence, to a single key driver or intervention at a time. This allows for clear internal communication and a more direct connection between feedback and action. But does it do so at the risk of generating apathy among those employees who may have expressed concern about another, unaddressed theme?

While technologies have enabled us to more easily and frequently measure engagement, there also has been a rapid advancement of tools and applications that go beyond collecting survey data. The use of hand held and wearable technologies and other innovative tools has opened the possibility to move beyond simply asking employees about their levels of satisfaction, commitment, and engagement, and measure those concepts more directly. In his 2015 review of advanced wearable technologies and their impact on multiple areas of work and life, Adam Thierer (2015) notes that despite the concerns of privacy and security, connected devices and applications can make lives easier, safer, healthier, and more productive. Although health and fitness and home or task automation usage has seen the largest adoption in this area, the possibilities are growing around usage for workplace safety, productivity, and social interaction or networking tracking. However, in order to use a more direct and multi-method approach for measuring engagement, satisfaction, and commitment, it is important to link behaviors, communication, and actions to the constructs that are widely accepted today. If an employee's activity during the day results in 5,000 movements but their coworker who is more productive than they are, only makes 4,000 movements, does that tell us something about engagement with their work?

Similarly, the more prevalent use of social networking applications, can provide insights into the interactions people have regularly at work, how those interactions may influence their available resources, or perhaps their embeddedness in the organization. For example, if an employee joins and is an active member of five or more online, internal special interest communities, does that mean they are more engaged with the organization? There has been growing interest in the use of social network analysis in the study of group behavior and social influence (Wolfer, Faber, and Hewstone 2015). The improved ability to collect that data opens up the potential for this rich information about human interactions at work to be applied more rigorously to the study of worker engagement.

Identifying other, technologically based measurement methods and tools, to enhance traditional surveys, can result in our ability to fill in some of the gaps that still exist in effectively and accurately capturing individual, team, and organizational levels of engagement. Multi-level models of efficacy that examine engagement, longitudinally, within the broader organizational context need rigorous validation. Rather than recommend organizations focus on the drivers with the strongest effect sizes, as has traditionally been the case, perhaps there is a better alternative that continues to balance the need for employee agency against targeted and resource-constrained organizational change initiatives.

Consistent with the personal shift and adoption of advanced technologies to enhance individuals' lives, most organizations have also moved away from more manual and paper-based methods of managing their workforce to the use of automated, advanced, and networked systems. In particular, there has been rapid advancement of applications and technology for human capital and talent management. The movement toward cloud-based, SaaS technology makes these tools more accessible than they ever have before. With these advanced tools, which cross over multiple areas of human capital management, the ability to capture key metrics and link them back to engagement measurements is just beginning to take shape. Since many actions and initiatives to improve engagement are directly related to talent management practices such as talent acquisition, on-boarding, learning, development, compensation, performance feedback, and talent mobility/succession, it only makes sense that this data should be leveraged to further explore the linkages to employee engagement in a broader model. Jiang et al. (2012) proposed a theoretical model based on a meta-analytic study of the effects of various human capital practices and dimensions on organizational outcomes. Models such as this indicate the key role of employee engagement, satisfaction, commitment, and citizenship behavior on key performance indicators. As a result, proactively measuring monitoring those indicators which are incorporated into the talent management system, and within the control of managers, as predictors of engagement allows organizations to put their efforts, energy, time, money, and resources into the most critical solutions for their workforce and the company as a whole.

Talent management professionals have traditionally exerted tight control over employee feedback results to protect confidentiality and to allow for human analysis and interpretation of the data prior to broadly communicating results. As the volume of data increases and the flow of feedback to managers and employees increases, they become more empowered. But the risk of misinterpretation also increases. How do we ensure statistically significant but practically meaningless fluctuations do not cause unnecessary heartburn in the workplace? Advances in data visualization are and will continue to be an area of innovation in the field. Sifting through the noise, providing context for results, and focusing those who may have little or no background in statistics on meaningful results and recommended actions can help to further the feedback loop.

When every manager has the tools and capability to respond to their team's feedback, how often should they do so? What additional training and tools are needed to help managers focus on the most impactful interventions? Oversampling and survey fatigue continue to be real concerns. What is the optimal relationship between polling frequency, question volume, and statistically representative results? Researchers have an opportunity to inform practitioners in this area as well.

Finally, since many of the drivers of engagement relate back to human capital practices--employee development, career growth, performance alignment, relationship with one's manager--could the use of talent management systems be a conduit to improving engagement? These systems allow employees to more easily manage their work and career and provide managers with well-defined, real time tools for providing feedback, delivering training, and monitoring results. When organizations fully leverage this technology, will it have a positive impact on engagement?

CLOSING THOUGHTS

These are exciting times for researchers and practitioners of employee engagement, satisfaction, and organizational commitment. Technology has in many ways democratized the field and will continue to do so. Techniques popularized in other fields such as marketing and customer research, coupled with general trends towards consumerization, have also greatly expanded the tools available for collecting employee feedback and connecting it to business outcomes. Whether through traditional, direct measures or more passive, non-intrusive methods, it is becoming easier to gauge the extent to which individuals, teams, and organizations are engaged, satisfied, and committed.

As tools for measuring feedback multiply, the frequency of data collection increases, and machine learning and black box algorithms advance in sophistication, we must hold ourselves to a high standard of explanation and reproducibility. Practitioners and providers will continue to throw new techniques and methods at the topic that may be sorely lacking in vigorous research. The individual level of analysis, traditionally off-limits and considered private or confidential, is poised to become more open and accessible. How best to make employee engagement an inclusive and open topic for employees who may otherwise be quite content completing surveys and sharing their personality dimensions on social media? Techniques borrowed from gamification may present opportunities for researchers to further examine the individual level of analysis. Opt-in, self-identification may be a solution, so long as employees see sufficient value in the results and do not fear retaliation from their supervisors. As the calculations underlying results and driver analysis become more abstract, we will need to develop intuitive approaches for summarizing vast datasets to both technical and non-technical audiences.

Accessing data and separating "digital exhaust" from practically significant findings will continue to pose a challenge. On the one hand, we live in an age of big data where just about anything seems possible from a methodological and statistical point of view. Yet, as data is collected at an exponential rate, it also risks being misinterpreted or becoming ensconced behind digital gates. In many ways, this can be seen a positive development--increased public awareness of privacy personal and digital security has generally led to many consumer- and employee-friendly regulations, wider availability of data encryption, implementation of information security best practices, and responsible handling of personally identifiable information. However, researchers and practitioners will need to work ever harder to test innovative new theories against data that may now be off-limits or only accessible through multiple rounds of institutional, organizational, and legal review. The reward is great--data that can test and refine multi-level models of engagement--but it will be reserved for the persistent.

Though it is no surprise that feedback tied to action can drive behavior, organizations have traditionally struggled to do just that when it comes to employee engagement. Technology has enabled exciting new tools to help employers finally reach toward that goal, but many practical considerations remain. Implementing advanced models of employee engagement to improve individual, team, and organizational outcomes will continue to require not only precise feedback and analysis, but also organizational awareness, understanding, and willingness to embrace change. Employee engagement is not merely a one-time problem to be solved, but an integrated, continuous way of thinking.

ACKNOWLEDGEMENTS

The authors thank EIASM for organizing the Workshop for Strategic Human Resource Management that provided the opportunity to engage in this discussion. We also thank the French Investissements d'Avenir (ANR-11-IDEX-0003/Labex Ecodec/ANR-11-LABX-0047) for funding our working meetings to produce this article. Additionally, we thank HEC Paris School of Management and NEOMA Business School for their support of our research.

REFERENCES

Albrecht, S. L. 2010. *Handbook of Employee Engagement: Perspectives, issues, research and Practice.* Northampton, MA: Edward Elgar.

Albrecht, S. L., A. B. Bakker, J. A. Gruman, W. H. Macey, and A. M. Saks. 2015. "Employee Engagement, Human Resource Management Practices and Competitive Advantage: An Integrated Approach." *Journal of Organizational Effectiveness: People and Performance* 2 (1):7–35. doi: 10.1108/JOEPP-08-2014-0042.

Aon, Hewitt. 2013. Managing Employee Engagement During Times of Change. [PDF file] Aon Hewitt Human Capital Consulting. Retrieved from http://www.aon.com/attachments/human-capitalconsulting/2013_Managing_Engagement_During_Times_of_Change_White_Paper.pdf.

Aon, Hewitt. 2017. 2017 Trends in Global Employee Engagement: Global Anxiety Erodes Employee Engagement Gains. [PDF file]. Aon Hewitt. Retrieved from http://www.aon.com/engagement17/

Bakker, A. B. 2014. "Daily Fluctuations in Work Engagement: An Overview and Current Directions." *European Psychologist* 19 (4):227–36. doi: 10.1027/1016-9040/a000160.

Bakker, A. B., and P. M. Bal. 2010. "Weekly Work Engagement and Performance: A Study among Starting Teachers." *Journal of Occupational and Organizational Psychology* 83:180–206.

Bakker, A. B., H. Van Emmerik, and M. C. Euwema. 2006. "Crossover of Burnout and Engagement in Work Teams." *Work and Occupations* 33 (4):464–89. doi: 10.1177/0730888406291310.

Christian, M. S., A. S. Garza, and J. E. Slaughter. 2011. "Work Engagement: A Quantitative Review and Test of Its Relations with Task and Contextual Performance." *Personnel Psychology* 64 (1):89–136. doi: 10.1111/j.1744-6570.2010.01203.x.

Cornerstone OnDemand. 2016. Toxic Employees in the Workplace: Hidden Costs and How to Spot Them. [PDF file]. Retrieved from www.cornerstoneondemand.com.

Deloitte. 2017. *2017 Deloitte Global Human Capital Trends Report.* [PDF file]. Deloitte University Press. Retrieved from https://www2.deloitte.com/us/en/pages/human-capital/articles/introduction-human-capital-trends.html.

Harter, J. D., F. L. Schmidt, S. Agrawal, S. K. Plowman, and A. Blue. 2016. *The Relationship between Engagement at Work and Organizational Outcomes: 2016 Q12 Meta-Analysis.* 9th Ed. Washington D.C.: Gallup, Inc.

Jiang, K., D. P. Lepak, J. Hu, and J. C. Baer. 2012. "How Does Human Resource Management Influence Organizational Outcomes? A Meta-analytic Investigation of Mediating Mechanisms." *Academy of Management Journal* 55 (6):1264–94. doi: 10.5465/amj.2011.0088.

Macey, W. H., B. Schneider, K. M. Barbera, and S. A. Young. 2009. *Employee Engagement: Tools for Analysis, practice, and Competitive Advantage.* New York, NY: Wiley-Blackwell.

Pierce, J. R., and H. Aguinis. 2013. "The Too-Much-of-a-Good-Thing Effect in Management." *Journal of Management* 39 (2):313–38. doi: 10.1177/0149206311410060.

Schaufeli, W. B., A. B. Bakker, and M. Salanova. 2006. "The Measurement of Work Engagement with a Short Questionnaire: A Cross-national Study." *Educational and Psychological Measurement* 66 (4):701–16. doi: 10.1177/0013164405282471.

Silvis, P. 2016. Why Employee Engagement Still Matters. [PDF file] Greenleaf Center for Servant Leadership. Retrieved from https://www.greenleaf.org/winning-workplaces/workplace-resources/features/workplace-perspectives/why-employee-engagement-still-matters/.

Sonnentag, S. 2003. "Recovery, Work Engagement, and Proactive Behavior: A New Look at the Interface between Nonwork and Work." *Journal of Applied Psychology* 88 (3):518–28. doi: 10.1037/0021-9010.88.3.518.

The Conference Board. 2006. Employee Engagement: A review of current research and its implications. [PDF file]. Retrieved from www.conference-board.org.

Thierer, A. D. 2015. "The Internet of Things and Wearable Technology: Addressing Privacy and Security Concerns without Derailing Innovation." *Richmond Journal of Law and Technology* 21 (2):1–118.

Wolfer, R., N. S. Faber, and M. Hewstone. 2015. "Social Network Analysis in the Science of Groups: Cross-sectional and Longitudinal Applications for Studying Intra- and Intergroup Behavior." *Group Dynamics: Theory, Research and Practice* 19 (1):45–61. doi: 10.1037/gdn0000021.

Index

Für Rückfragen steht Ihnen unser Informationsservice zur Verfügung:
Informationsservice CHEMetall GmbH, Abteilung Drucke, Lyoner Straße 9, 60528 Frankfurt
Verlag: GmbH, Reuterstraße 23, 80333 München Germany